Pocket Guide to Depression Glass

Revised Sixth Edition

By Gene Florence

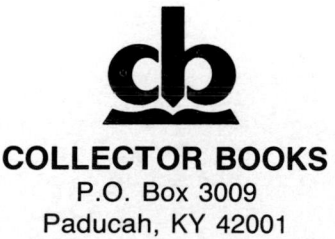

COLLECTOR BOOKS
P.O. Box 3009
Paducah, KY 42001

Notice

The current values in this book should be used only as a guide. They are not intended to set prices, which vary from one section of the country to another. Auction prices as well as dealer prices vary greatly and are affected by condition as well as demand. Neither the Author nor the Publisher assumes responsibility for any losses that might be incurred as a result of consulting this guide.

A listing of the colors to be found in each pattern is mentioned under the photo headings. However, the prices catalogued herein represent those colors most commonly collected in each pattern. See THE *Collector's Encyclopedia of Depression Glass* should you desire more detailed information.

FOREWORD

Depression Glass as defined in this book is the colored glassware made primarily during the Depression years in the colors of amber, green, pink, blue, red, yellow, white and crystal. There are other colors and some of the glassware included in this book was made later than the Depression era; but it has still been collected as that era glassware because of its color. The main emphasis of this book is given to the inexpensively made glassware produced in quantity and sold through the five and dime stores or given away as premiums or included with the purchase of other products, i.e. the spice shaker contained a certain brand spice.

Information for this book has come from over 750,000 miles of travel throughout the country in connection with glassware over the past seven years and from the research and sale of over 300,000 copies of the *Collector's Encyclopedia of Depression Glass*.

ACKNOWLEDGMENTS

I would like at this time to say a word of thanks to the people who generously lent their glassware to be photographed. They are as follows: Lois Florence, my sister, and my mother, Gladys Florence of Grannie Bear Antiques.

Also, a special thanks to my family for their support in various ways, gathering bits of information, taking over my responsibilities to leave me free to write. Again my wife, Cathy, struggled with my handwriting to serve as typist and editor for this little book. Anyone having seen my handwriting will realize this was no small task.

A special thanks to Tom Clouser, Curtis and Mays Photographic Studio & Gallery of Paducah, Kentucky for the photographs in the book.

PRICING

Glass that is in less than mint condition, i.e. chipped, cracked, scratched or poorly molded, will bring very small prices unless extremely rare; and then, will bring only a small percentage of the price of glass that is in mint condition.

This book is meant as a guide to price; however, if your Depression Glass comes to you at bargain rates or free from a relative, then that's all to the good!

Prices have become almost standardized due to national advertising by dealers and due to the Depression Glass Shows which are held from coast to coast. However, there are some regional differences in prices due to glass being more readily available in some areas of the country than in others. Too, companies distributed certain pieces in some areas that it did not in others.

CONTENTS

HOW TO FIND DEPRESSION GLASS

The best place to find Depression Glass is in your own basement, garage or attic—or even in your own cupboards. Yes, that's true. Nearly everyone has at least a piece or two around their own home; it may be a bowl that belonged to grandmother and got handed down; it may be a complete setting that an aunt or someone got as a wedding gift and packed away for storage in the attic.

First of all, you need to learn to recognize the colors Depression Glass comes in for often the coloring of the glass is recognizable as Depression era glassware even when the pattern name is yet unknown. That was primarily the reason for making this book a full color book so that the novice collector could acquaint himself with the full range of colors the glass may be found in.

Once you have searched your own shelves and those of your immediate relatives and friends, your next source for finding Depression Glass should be the garage sales, tag sales, yard sales, etc. where people are cleaning out their attics and garages. Don't forget the church bazaar, the Salvation Army store or the Volunteers of America. You'll find competition is keen at these latter places; so you'll need to shop early.

Now that you've covered all the afore mentioned places, it's time to make a tour of the antique and junk shops in your area. These are often gold mines of the ridiculous to the sublime price wise; so have in mind what you'll pay for a particular item. Too, most of these shops expect to haggle a bit over price; so don't be shy.

Household and estate auctions are often another valuable source for finding Depression Glass; but it is wise to check out the merchandise before making a bid as chips and small damage to an item may be overlooked by the harried auctioneer.

Many collectors feel that antique shows and flea markets are the very best places to find Depression Glass. So, don't forget to put these on your agenda.

I find my best sources for finding the particular pieces and patterns in Depression Glass are the Depression Glass Shows put on by clubs throughout the country and the publications which deal primarily in Depression era glass. You will find two of the best listed on page 159 of this book. There are other publications, of course; but for overall information and volume of advertisement of glass, I like these two.

SELLING

One of the purposes of this book is to help you make money from any of your unwanted glassware treasures; any number of books infer that there are treasures in your attic, but few tell you how to reap benefits from them. To find a reputable dealer in your area is not always an easy task; but here are a few suggestions. If you live in an area where a show is held regularly, watch for advertisements and attend the show. You might find a buyer for your glass among the dealers at the show. If there is a Depression Glass Club meeting in your area, there may be members there who would be willing to buy your glass or who could put you in contact with someone who would. Failing either of those methods, you could send for a sample copy of one of the publications listed at the end of the book and seek a dealer in your area by looking through the ads. The telephone directory or the ads under antiques in your local newspaper may lead you to a dealer in glass who would be interested in buying yours; or you might take it to a local flea market and find a buyer among the dealers set up there.

The prices herein are retail and you can expect to receive 50 to 70% of the prices listed for the popular, highly collectible patterns, but only 35 to 50% of prices listed for the patterns that are not as avidly sought by collectors.

There are several factors a dealer will consider when offering for your piece; its condition, how popular this color is with potential buyers, whether or not the pattern is one numerous people collect, whether he has plenty in stock already, or whether he thinks he can make money on the piece before he's had to pack it up at 65 different shows throughout the country and dropped it and broken it. Popularity of a pattern and the demand for it are the two key factors in interesting a potential buyer of your glassware. This book should give you an accurate guide as to what to expect for your glass. You shouldn't be walking up to a dealer without the faintest idea of what your glass is worth; neither should you expect him to pay you retail price for the glass if you're sincerely wanting him to buy it.

WHAT TO COLLECT —
HELPFUL HINT SECTION

Many beginning collectors make the mistake of trying to collect everything in sight; and unless you have a few oil wells on the side, you can soon find yourself out of funds doing this.

My first suggestion is to study this book. Most of you have looked at the pictures before even starting to read this; that's a start. You have a general idea of what's available. Decide on one or possibly two patterns you like; once you see it close at hand, you may change your mind; but that's all right. Collectors do that for a variety of reasons. However, it's wise to settle on something specific to look for rather than to pick and choose at random.

If money is a problem, pursue the prices of the various patterns and choose one that is less expensive to collect. However, you should become familiar with the whole range of patterns and you should have a general idea of the range of prices on the more expensive pieces of the patterns because everyone, sooner or later, stumbles onto a piece of glass worth $50.00 that's priced at $5.00; and even if you don't care for the piece or the pattern, you should go ahead and buy it because you'll either be able to trade it to someone who does want it for the pattern you want, or you can sell it and use the extra money to buy the glass you like.

In the early 1960s through the early 1970s, you could by Depression glass by the box and crate loads at auctions for a song; thus, you could afford to collect several patterns at once; however, those days have come to an end; so, it's better to have something definite in mind to collect.

If money is no problem, then by all means, choose one of the more expensive patterns to collect; as there are more people wanting these patterns usually, the market value of your pattern will be stable at the least, and will probably increase as the years pass.

Some people don't choose to collect an entire pattern; they collect one piece of every pattern, say plates; one California collector collects only cookie jars; another I know collects only candy jars; there are numerous salt and pepper collections; so you could choose to collect only one or two pieces of several patterns. In any case, you'll find the glass attractive to serve in and a real item of conversation.

If you are hard bitten by the bug of collecting Depression Glass, then you might possibly want a more detailed guide for the glass; should that happen, I'd be delighted to recommend my *Collector's Encyclopedia of Depression Glass*, which can be ordered from this publisher or myself. I receive letters daily from its delighted readers. In any case, happy hunting—and even happier finding. It's a hobby I think you'll not only enjoy but one from which you'll profit.

ADAM
(See Reproduction Section, Page 136)
(pink, green, crystal, yellow, delphite)
JEANNETTE GLASS COMPANY, 1932-1934

	Pink	Green		Pink	Green
Ash Tray, 4½″	23.00	17.50	Plate, 6″ Sherbet	4.00	4.50
Bowl, 4¾″ Dessert	10.00	10.00	Plate, 7¾″ Sq. Salad	8.00	8.50
Bowl, 5¾″ Cereal	30.00	30.00	Plate, 9″ Sq. Dinner	17.00	16.00
Bowl, 7¾″	15.00	15.00	Plate, 9″ Grill	14.00	13.00
Bowl, 9″ Covered	42.00	65.00	Platter, 11¾″	15.00	16.00
Bowl, 10″ Oval	16.00	19.00	Relish Dish, 8″ Divided . .	10.00	12.50
Butter Dish & Cover	65.00	250.00	Salt & Pepper, 4″	42.50	77.50
Cake Plate, 10″ Footed . .	14.00	17.00	Saucer, Sq. 6″	3.50	4.00
Candlesticks, 4″, Pr.	60.00	77.50	Sherbet, 3″	18.00	28.00
Candy Jar & Cover, 2½″ .	60.00	75.00	Sugar	12.00	15.00
Coaster, 3¾″	15.00	13.00	Sugar/Candy Cover	15.00	30.00
Creamer	13.00	14.00	Tumbler, 4½″	18.00	16.00
Cup	18.00	16.00	Tumbler, 5½″ Iced Tea . .	43.00	32.00
Lamp	225.00	225.00	Vase, 7½″	175.00	35.00
Pitcher, 8″, 32 oz.	25.00	32.50			

AMERICAN PIONEER
(pink, green, amber, crystal)
LIBERTY WORKS, 1931-1934

	Pink	Green
Bowl, 5″ Handled	12.50	15.00
Bowl, 8¾″ Covered	70.00	85.00
Bowl, 9″ Handled	15.00	20.00
Bowl, Console, 10⅜″	40.00	50.00
✗ Candlesticks, 6½″, Pr. . . .	50.00	65.00
Candy Jar & Cover, 1 lb. .	65.00	85.00
Candy Jar & Cover, 1½ lb.	75.00	95.00
Cheese & Cracker Set (indented platter & compote)	35.00	45.00
Coaster, 3½″	15.00	18.00
Creamer, 2¾	15.00	18.00
Creamer, 3½″	16.00	17.50
Cup	7.00	9.00
Dresser Set (2 cologne, powder jar, on indented 7½″ tray)	175.00	250.00
Goblet, Wine, 4″, 3 oz. . . .	30.00	40.00
Goblet, Water, 6″, 8 oz. . .	27.00	33.00
Ice Bucket, 6″	35.00	42.00

	Pink	Green
Lamp, 8½″ Tall.	75.00	95.00
Mayonnaise, 4¼″	45.00	75.00
Pitcher, 5″ Covered Urn . .	110.00	145.00
Pitcher, 7″ Covered Urn . .	130.00	175.00
Plate, 6″	8.00	10.00
Plate, 6″ Handled	8.00	10.00
Plate, 8″	6.00	7.00
Plate, 11½″ Handled	10.00	14.00
Saucer	3.00	4.00
Sherbet, 3½″	12.00	16.00
Sherbet, 4¾″	22.00	30.00
Sugar, 2¾″	15.00	17.00
Sugar, 3½″	16.00	17.50
Tumbler, 5 oz. Juice	17.50	22.50
Tumbler, 4″, 8 oz.	20.00	27.50
Tumbler, 5″, 12 oz.	25.00	40.00
Vase, 7″, three styles, rolled or crimped edge, straight	60.00	77.50
Whiskey, 2¼″, 2 oz.	32.50	65.00

AMERICAN SWEETHEART
(pink, monax, cremax, red and blue)
MacBETH-EVANS GLASS COMPANY, 1930-1936

	Pink	Monax		Pink	Monax
Bowl, 3¾" Flat, Berry . . .	25.00	----	Plate, 15½"	----	165.00
Bowl, 4½" Cream Soup . .	30.00	40.00	Platter, 13" Oval	20.00	40.00
Bowl, 6" Cereal	9.50	8.50	Pitcher, 7½", 60 oz.	395.00	----
Bowl, 9" Round, Berry . . .	22.00	38.00	Pitcher, 8", 80 oz.	360.00	----
Bowl, 9½" Flat Soup	29.00	40.00	Salt & Pepper, Footed . . .	275.00	200.00
Bowl, 11" Oval Vegetable	32.00	40.00	Saucer	2.50	1.50
Bowl, 18" Console	----	275.00	Sherbet, Footed, 3¾" . . .	12.00	----
Creamer, Footed	8.00	7.50	Sherbet, Footed, 4¼" . . .	10.00	13.00
Cup	9.50	7.00	Sugar, Open, Footed	7.50	5.00
Plate, 6" Bread & Butter .	2.00	3.00	Sugar Cover	----	155.00
Plate, 8" Salad	7.00	6.00	Tumbler, 3½", 5 oz.	40.00	----
Plate, 9" Luncheon	----	8.00	Tumbler, 4¼", 9 oz.	45.00	----
Plate, 9¾"-10¼" Dinner .	15.00	12.50	Tumbler, 4¾", 10 oz.	52.00	----
Plate, 12" Salver	9.00	9.00			

ANNIVERSARY
(pink) (recently in crystal and iridescent)
JEANNETTE GLASS COMPANY, 1947-1949

	Crystal	Pink		Crystal	Pink
Bowl, 4⅞″ Berry	1.50	3.00	Plate, 9″ Dinner	3.50	5.50
Bowl, 7⅜″ Soup	4.00	10.00	Plate, 12½″ Sandwich		
Bowl, 9″ Fruit	7.00	14.00	Server	4.00	7.50
Butter Dish & Cover	22.50	45.00	Relish Dish, 8″	4.50	7.50
Candy Jar & Cover	17.50	30.00	Saucer	1.00	1.50
Compote, Open, 3 Legged	3.50	8.00	Sherbet, Footed	2.50	5.50
Cake Plate, 12½″	5.50	10.00	Sugar	2.00	5.00
Cake Plate with Cover	10.00	13.00	Sugar Cover	5.00	7.50
Creamer, Footed	3.50	7.50	Vase, 6½″	9.00	15.00
Cup	3.50	4.50	Vase, Wall Pin-up	10.00	16.00
Pickle Dish, 9″	3.50	7.00	Wine Glass, 2½ oz.	5.00	11.00
Plate, 6¼″ Sherbet	1.25	2.00			

AUNT POLLY
(green, blue, iridescent)
U.S. GLASS COMPANY, Late 1920s

	Green	Blue		Green	Blue
Bowl, 4⅜″ Berry	6.00	10.00	Pitcher, 8″, 48 oz.	----	135.00
Bowl, 4¾″, 2″ High	8.50	14.00	Plate, 6″ Sherbet	4.00	6.00
Bowl, 7¼″ Oval, Handled			Plate, 8″ Luncheon	----	12.00
Pickle	9.00	18.00	Salt and Pepper	----	160.00
Bowl, 7⅞″ Large Berry	15.00	22.00	Sherbet	7.50	8.50
Bowl, 8⅜″ Oval	30.00	50.00	Sugar	20.00	25.00
Butter Dish & Cover	200.00	160.00	Sugar Cover	40.00	75.00
Candy, Cover, Two Handled	35.00	50.00	Tumbler, 3⅝″, 8 oz.	----	20.00
Creamer	22.00	33.00	Vase, 6½″, Footed	22.50	30.00

AURORA
(cobalt)
HAZEL ATLAS COMPANY, 1937-1938

	Cobalt		Cobalt
Bowl, 4½″	15.00	Plate, 6½″	4.00
Bowl, 5⅜″	8.00	Saucer	2.50
Creamer, 4½″	10.00	Tumbler, 4¾″	13.00
Cup	6.00		

AVOCADO, "SWEET PEAR", No. 601
(See Reproduction Section, Page 137)
(pink, green)
INDIANA GLASS COMPANY, 1923-1933

	Pink	Green
Bowl, 5¼", Two-Handled	20.00	23.00
Bowl, 6" Relish, Footed .	15.00	20.00
Bowl, 7" Preserve, One Handle	13.00	16.00
Bowl, 7½" Salad	25.00	40.00
Bowl, 8" Oval, Two-Handled	15.00	20.00
Bowl, 9½", 3¼" Deep . .	65.00	85.00
*Creamer, Footed	25.00	27.50
Cup, Footed	25.00	26.00

	Pink	Green
Pitcher, 64 ozs.	425.00	695.00
*Plate, 6¾" Sherbet	9.50	11.50
Plate, 8¼" Luncheon . . .	13.00	15.00
Plate, 10¼" Two Handled Cake	25.00	35.00
Saucer	18.00	20.00
*Sherbet	40.00	45.00
*Sugar, Footed	25.00	27.50
Tumbler	85.00	135.00

*Recently made in green

BEADED BLOCK
(pink, green, crystal, ice blue, vaseline, iridescent, amber, opalescent colors)
IMPERIAL GLASS COMPANY, 1927-1930s

	Green	Opale-scent		Green	Opale-scent
Bowl, 4½″, 2 Handled Jelly	6.00	12.50	Bowl, 7½″, Round, Plain		
Bowl, 4½″, Round, Lily ..	8.50	15.00	Edge	7.50	13.50
Bowl, 5½″, Square	6.00	8.50	Bowl, 8¼″, Celery	9.00	15.00
Bowl, 5½″, 1 Handle	6.50	10.00	Creamer	12.50	20.00
Bowl, 6″, Deep, Round ..	8.50	15.00	Pitcher, 5¼″, Pint Jug . . .	75.00	---
Bowl, 6¼″, Round	6.50	14.00	Plate, 7¾″ Sq.	5.00	9.00
Bowl, 6½″, Round	6.50	14.00	Plate, 8¾″, Round	10.00	15.00
Bowl, 6½″, 2 Handled			Stemmed Jelly, 4½″	8.00	15.00
Pickle	10.00	15.00	Stemmed Jelly, 4½″,		
Bowl, 6¾″ Round, Unflared	8.50	12.50	Flared Top	9.00	16.00
Bowl, 7¼″, Round, Flared	8.00	15.00	Sugar	12.50	20.00
Bowl, 7½″, Round Fluted			Vase, 6″, Bouquet	10.00	18.00
Edges	17.50	20.00			

BLOCK OPTIC, "BLOCK"
(green, yellow, pink, crystal)
HOCKING GLASS COMPANY, 1929-1933

	Pink	Green		Pink	Green
Bowl, 4¼" Berry	4.50	5.00	Plate, 8" Luncheon	2.50	3.00
Bowl, 5¼" Cereal	6.00	9.00	Plate, 9" Dinner	17.00	13.50
Bowl, 7¼" Salad	12.00	15.00	Salt & Pepper, Footed	45.00	22.50
Bowl, 8½" Large Berry	12.00	15.00	Salt & Pepper, Squatty	----	50.00
Butter Dish & Cover, 3"x5"	----	37.50	Sandwich Server, Center		
Candlesticks, 1¾", Pr.	40.00	50.00	Handle	35.00	40.00
Candy Jar & Cover,			Saucer, 2 Sizes, Cup Ring	5.00	7.00
2¼" Tall	32.50	30.00	Sherbet, Non-Stemmed		
Candy Jar Cover, 6¼" Tall	50.00	37.50	(Cone)	----	3.00
Compote, 4" Wide			Sherbet, 3¼", 5½ oz.	6.00	4.50
Mayonnaise	42.00	22.00	Sherbet, 4¾", 6 oz.	9.00	11.00
Creamer, Three Styles:			Sugar, Three Styles: As		
Cone Shaped, Round			Creamer	8.00	9.00
Footed & Flat	9.50	10.00	Tumbler, 3½", 5 oz. Flat	12.00	11.00
Cup, Four Styles	4.00	5.00	Tumbler, 4", 5 oz. Footed	12.00	15.00
Goblet, 4" Cocktail	20.00	19.00	Tumbler, 9 oz. Flat	10.00	10.00
Goblet, 4½", Wine	20.00	19.00	Tumbler, 9 oz. Footed	11.50	13.50
Goblet, 5¾", 9 oz.	13.00	17.00	Tumbler, 10 oz. Flat	11.00	14.00
Ice Bucket	22.50	27.50	Tumbler, 6", 10 oz. Footed	15.00	16.00
Ice Tub or Butter Tub, Open	65.00	27.00	Tumbler, 14 oz. Flat	----	20.00
Mug, Flat Creamer,			Tumble-up Night Set: 3"		
No Spout	----	25.00	Tumbler Bottle & Tumbler,		
Pitcher, 7⅝", 68 oz.	40.00	55.00	6" High	----	45.00
Pitcher, 8½", 54 oz.	27.50	25.00	Vase, 5¾" Blown	----	150.00
Pitcher, 8", 80 oz.	45.00	37.50	Whiskey, 2¼", 2 oz.	16.00	16.00
Plate, 6" Sherbet	1.50	1.50			

"BOWKNOT"
(green)
UNKNOWN MANUFACTURER

	Green		Green
Bowl, 4½″ Berry	9.00	Sherbet, Low Footed	9.00
Bowl, 5½″ Cereal	12.00	Tumbler, 5″, 10 oz.	11.00
Cup	5.00	Tumbler, 5″, 10 oz. Footed	11.00
Plate, 7″ Salad	7.50		

"BUBBLE", "FIRE KING"
(blue, dark green, ruby red, crystal)
HOCKING GLASS COMPANY, 1934-1965

	Crystal	Blue		Crystal	Blue
Bowl, 4" Berry	3.50	10.00	Plate, 9⅜" Dinner	3.50	5.00
Bowl, 4½" Fruit	2.00	7.00	Platter, 12" Oval	4.00	11.00
Bowl, 5¼" Cereal	3.00	8.00	Saucer	.50	1.00
Bowl, 7¾" Flat Soup	5.00	9.00	Sugar	3.00	12.50
Bowl, 8⅜" Large Berry	4.00	9.00	Tumbler, 6 oz. Juice (Red)	----	6.50
Creamer	3.50	21.00	Tumbler, 9 oz. Water (Red)	----	6.00
Cup	2.00	3.00	Tumbler, 12 oz. Iced Tea		
Pitcher, 64 oz., Ice Lip (Red)		37.50	(Red)	----	9.00
Plate, 6¾" Bread & Butter	1.00	2.00	Tumbler, 16 oz. Lemonade		
Plate, 9⅜" Grill	----	12.00	(Red)	----	15.00

CAMEO, "BALLERINA," or "DANCING GIRL"
(green, yellow, pink and crystal with a platinum rim)
HOCKING GLASS COMPANY, 1930-1934

	Green	Yellow		Green	Yellow
Bowl, 4¾" Cream Soup	45.00	----	Decanter, 10" w/Stopper	95.00	----
Bowl, 5½" Cereal	22.00	23.00	Decanter, 10" w/Stopper,		
Bowl, 7¼" Salad	35.00	----	Frosted (Stoppers Repre-		
Bowl, 8¼" Large Berry	24.00	----	sent ½ Value of Decanter)	25.00	----
Bowl, 9" Rimmed Soup	28.00	----	Domino Tray, 7" w/3"		
Bowl, 10" Oval Vegetable	14.00	30.00	Indentation	77.50	----
Bowl, 11" 3 Leg Console	40.00	55.00	Goblet, 3½" Wine	350.00	----
Butter Dish & Cover	150.00	900.00	Goblet, 4" Wine	47.50	----
Cake Plate, 10" 3 Legs	15.00	----	Goblet, 6" Water	37.50	----
Candlesticks, 4" Pr.	75.00	----	Ice Bowl or Open Butter		
Candy Jar, Low 4" Cover	45.00	60.00	3" Tall x 5½" Wide	125.00	----
Candy Jar, 6½" Tall &			Jam Jar, 2" & Cover	120.00	----
Cover	95.00	----	Pitcher, 5¾" Syrup or Milk,		
Cocktail Shaker (Metal Lid)			20 oz.	145.00	450.00
Appears in Crystal Only	----	400.00	Pitcher, 6" Juice, 36 oz.	42.50	----
Compote, 4" Wide			Pitcher, 8½" Water, 56 oz.	37.50	----
Mayonnaise	21.00	----	Plate, 6" Sherbet	2.00	2.00
Cookie Jar & Cover	37.50	----	Plate, 8" Luncheon	7.50	7.50
Creamer, 3¼"	16.50	12.50	Plate, 8½" Square	27.50	125.00
Creamer, 4¼"	17.50	----	Plate, 9½" Dinner	12.00	6.50
Cup, Two Styles	11.00	6.50	Plate, 10" Sandwich	10.00	----

Plate, 10½" Grill	7.50	6.50
Plate, 10½" Grill w/Closed Handles	50.00	6.00
Plate, 10½" w/Closed Handles	7.00	6.00
Platter, 12" Closed Handles	14.00	28.00
Relish, 3 Part, 7½" Footed	20.00	125.00
Salt & Pepper, Footed, Pr.	50.00	----
Sandwich Server, Center Handle	2500.00	----
Saucer w/Cup Ring	87.50	----
Saucer, 6" (Sherbet Plate)	2.00	2.00
Sherbet, 3⅛"	10.00	25.00
Sherbet, 4⅞"	24.00	30.00
Sugar, 3¼"	11.50	10.00
Sugar, 4¼"	17.50	----
Tumbler, 3¾", 5 oz. Juice	21.50	----
Tumbler, 4", 9 oz. Water	18.00	----
Tumbler, 4¾", 10 oz. Flat	20.00	----
Tumbler, 5", 11 oz. Flat	20.00	37.50
Tumbler, 5¼", 15 oz.	45.00	----
Tumbler, 3 oz. Footed Juice	42.50	----
Tumbler, 5", 9 oz. Footed	19.00	12.00
Tumbler, 5¾", 11 oz. Footed	42.50	----
Vase, 5¾"	125.00	----
Vase, 8"	17.50	----
Water Bottle (Dark Green) Whitehouse Vinegar	15.00	----

CHERRY BLOSSOM
(See Reproduction Section, Page 138)   (pink, green, delphite, crystal)
JEANNETTE GLASS COMPANY, 1930-1939

	Pink	Green
Bowl, 4¾" Berry	9.00	12.00
Bowl, 5¾" Cereal	22.00	25.00
Bowl, 7¾" Flat Soup	37.50	40.00
Bowl, 8½" Round Berry . .	20.00	20.00
Bowl, 9" Oval Vegetable .	20.00	20.00
Bowl, 9" 2-Handled	14.00	16.00
Bowl, 10½", 3 Leg Fruit .	40.00	42.00
Butter Dish & Cover	55.00	65.00
Cake Plate (3 Legs) 10¼"	15.00	16.00
Coaster	10.00	9.00
Creamer	11.00	13.00
Cup	13.50	16.00
Mug, 7 oz.	160.00	180.00
Pitcher, 6¾" AOP, 36 oz. Scalloped or Round Bottom	30.00	38.00
Pitcher, 8" PAT, 36 oz. Ftd.	37.00	44.00
Pitcher, 8" PAT, 42 oz. Flat	32.00	40.00
Plate, 6" Sherbet	5.00	5.00
Plate, 7" Salad	13.00	15.00
Plate, 9" Dinner	12.00	14.00
Plate, 9" Grill	16.50	18.00
Platter, 9" Oval	650.00	----
Platter, 11" Oval	18.00	22.00
Platter, 13" & 13" Divided	35.00	40.00
Salt & Pepper Scalloped Bottom	1000.00	700.00

	Pink	Green
Saucer	2.50	3.00
Sherbet	10.00	12.00
Sugar	10.00	11.00
Sugar Cover	10.00	11.00
Tray, 10½" Sandwich, 2 Handled	10.00	12.00
Tumbler, 3¾", 4 oz. Footed, AOP, Round or Scalloped	11.00	14.00
Tumbler, 4½", 9 oz. Round Foot AOP	22.00	26.00
Tumbler, 4½", 8 oz. Scalloped Foot AOP . . .	24.00	28.00
Tumbler, 3½", 4 oz. Flat PAT	13.00	20.00
Tumbler, 4¼", 9 oz. Flat PAT	13.00	17.00
Tumbler, 5", 12 oz. Flat PAT	38.00	50.00

CHERRY BLOSSOM
CHILD'S JUNIOR DINNER SET

	Pink
Creamer	27.50
Sugar	27.50
Original Box	15.00
Plate, 6"	7.00
Cup	22.00
Saucer	3.50
14 Piece Set	195.00

CHINEX CLASSIC
(ivory, ivory decorated)
MacBETH-EVANS DIVISION OF CORNING GLASS WORKS,
Late 1930 - Early 1940s

	Ivory	Deco-rated		Ivory	Deco-rated
Bowl, 5¾" Cereal	4.00	5.00	Plate, 6¼" Sherbet	1.50	2.50
Bowl, 7" Salad	12.00	17.00	Plate, 9¾" Dinner	3.50	5.00
Bowl, 7¾" Flat Soup	11.00	15.00	Plate, 11½" Sandwich or		
Bowl, 9" Vegetable	9.50	12.50	Cake	6.50	10.00
Butter Dish	40.00	50.00	Saucer	1.50	2.50
Creamer	4.50	7.00	Sherbet, Low Footed	6.50	9.00
Cup	3.50	4.50	Sugar, Open	4.00	8.00

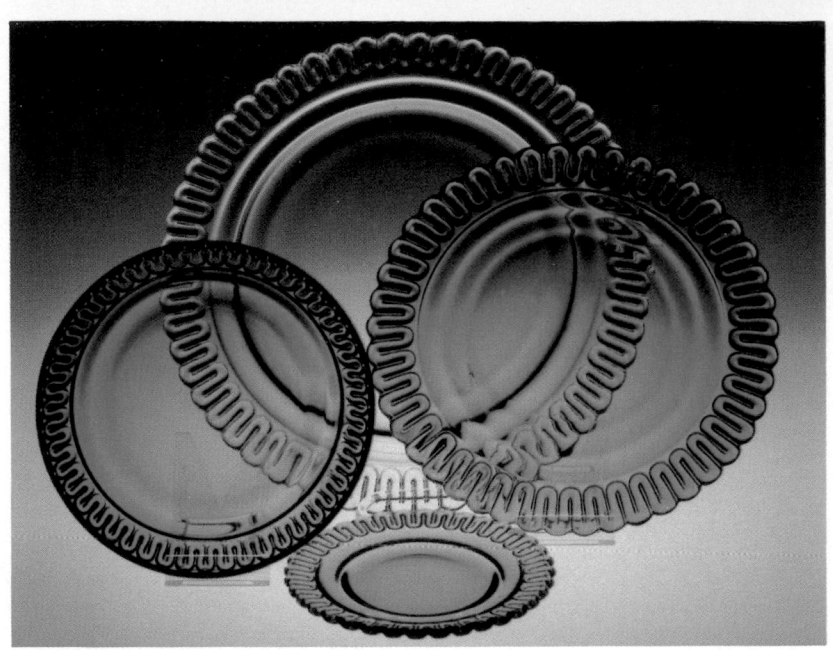

CHRISTMAS CANDY
(crystal, teal)
INDIANA GLASS COMPANY, 1950s

		Teal			Teal
Bowl, 7⅜" Soup	5.00	17.50	Plate, 9⅝" Dinner	7.00	20.00
Creamer	6.50	13.00	Plate, 11¼" Sandwich	10.00	27.50
Cup	3.50	12.00	Saucer	1.50	3.00
Plate, 6" Bread & Butter	2.50	8.00	Sugar	6.50	13.00
Plate, 8¼" Luncheon	5.50	13.00			

CIRCLE
(green, pink, crystal)
HOCKING GLASS COMPANY, 1930s

	Green or Pink		Green or Pink
Bowl, 4½"	3.25	Plate, 8¼" Luncheon	3.50
Bowl, 5½" Flared	5.00	Plate, 9½" Dinner	6.00
Bowl, 8"	7.50	Saucer	1.00
Creamer	5.00	Sherbet, 3⅛"	3.50
Cup	3.00	Sherbet, 4¾"	5.00
Goblet, 4½" Wine	4.50	Sugar	5.00
Goblet, 8 oz. Water	7.50	Tumbler, 4 oz. Juice	4.00
Pitcher, 80 oz.	17.50	Tumbler, 8 oz. Water	5.00
Plate, 6" Sherbet	2.00		

CLOVERLEAF
(pink, green, yellow, black)
HAZEL ATLAS GLASS COMPANY, 1930-1936

	Green	Yellow		Green	Yellow
Ash Tray 4″, Match Holder in Center (black only) . .	57.50	----	Plate, 6″ Sherbet	3.50	5.00
Ash Tray 5¾″, Match Holder in Center (black only)	70.00	----	Plate, 8″ Luncheon	5.00	10.50
			Plate, 10¼″ Grill	15.00	17.50
			Salt & Pepper, Pr.	22.50	85.00
			Saucer	2.50	3.00
Bowl, 4″ Dessert	12.50	17.50	Sherbet, 3″ Footed	4.50	8.50
Bowl, 5″ Cereal	20.00	20.00	Sugar, Footed, 3⅝″	7.50	12.50
Bowl, 7″ Salad	30.00	35.00	Tumbler, 3¾″, 9 oz. Flat .	30.00	----
Bowl, 8″	45.00	----	Tumbler, 4″, 10 oz Flat . .	28.00	----
Candy Dish & Cover	40.00	90.00	Tumbler, 5¾″, 10 oz. Footed	16.00	20.00
Creamer, Footed 3⅝″ . . .	7.50	12.50			
Cup	6.00	8.00			

COLONIAL, "KNIFE AND FORK"
(pink, green, crystal)
HOCKING GLASS COMPANY, 1934-1938

	Pink	Green		Pink	Green
Bowl, 3¾"	25.00	----	Plate, 6" Sherbet	3.50	4.00
Bowl, 4½" Berry	7.00	9.00	Plate, 8½" Luncheon	6.00	7.00
Bowl, 5½" Cereal	35.00	50.00	Plate, 10" Dinner	30.00	47.50
Bowl, 4½" Cream Soup . .	38.00	42.00	Plate, 10" Grill	17.50	20.00
Bowl, 7" Low Soup	35.00	40.00	Platter, 12" Oval	20.00	16.00
Bowl, 9" Large Berry	14.00	21.00	Salt & Pepper, Pr.	100.00	110.00
Bowl, 10" Oval Vegetable	20.00	22.00	Saucer (Same as sherbet		
Butter Dish & Cover	450.00	45.00	plate)	3.50	4.00
Creamer, 5", 8 oz.			Sherbet	7.50	11.00
(Milk Pitcher)	13.50	14.50	Spoon Holder or Celery . .	85.00	90.00
Cup	9.00	9.00	Sugar, 5"	15.00	11.00
Goblet, 3¾", 1 oz. Cordial	----	25.00	Sugar Cover	25.00	15.00
Goblet, 4", 3 oz. Cocktail .	----	20.00	Tumbler, 3", 5 oz. Juice . .	11.00	20.00
Goblet, 4½", 2½ oz. Wine	----	20.00	Tumbler, 4", 9 oz. Water .	10.00	16.00
Goblet, 5¼", 4 oz. Claret .	----	20.00	Tumbler, 10 oz.	25.00	33.00
Goblet, 5¾", 8½ oz. Water	----	22.50	Tumbler, 12 oz. Iced Tea .	33.00	42.00
Mug, 4½", 12 oz.	350.00	650.00	Tumbler, 15 oz. Lemonade	45.00	65.00
Pitcher, 7", 54 oz. Ice Lip			Tumbler, 3¼", 3 oz. Footed	10.00	14.00
or None	37.50	40.00	Tumbler, 4", 5 oz. Footed	15.00	22.50
Pitcher, 7¾", 68 oz. Ice Lip			Tumbler, 5¼", 10 oz. Ftd.	25.00	35.00
or None	45.00	50.00	Whiskey, 2½", 1½ oz. . . .	7.00	9.00

COLONIAL BLOCK
(green, pink, crystal, white)
HAZEL ATLAS GLASS COMPANY, Late 1920s - Early 1930s

	Green or Pink		Green or Pink
Bowl, 4″	5.00	Creamer	8.50
Bowl, 7″	12.50	Pitcher	27.50
Butter Dish	30.00	Sugar	9.00
Butter Tub	30.00	Sugar Cover	6.00
Candy Dish & Cover, 8½″	27.50		

COLONIAL FLUTED, ''ROPE''
(green, crystal)
FEDERAL GLASS COMPANY, 1928-1933

	Green		Green
Bowl, 4″ Berry	4.00	Plate, 6″ Sherbet	1.50
Bowl, 6″ Cereal	6.00	Plate, 8″ Luncheon	3.25
Bowl, 6½″ Deep Salad	13.00	Saucer	1.00
Bowl, 7½″ Large Berry	10.00	Sherbet	4.50
Creamer	4.50	Sugar	3.00
Cup	3.50	Sugar Cover	8.00

COLUMBIA
(crystal, pink)
FEDERAL GLASS COMPANY, 1938-1942

	Crystal	Pink		Crystal	Pink
Bowl, 5″ Cereal	10.00	----	Plate, 6″ Bread & Butter .	1.50	7.50
Bowl, 8″ Low Soup	11.00	----	Plate, 9½″ Luncheon	4.00	17.50
Bowl, 8½″ Salad	11.00	----	Plate, 11¾″ Chop	6.00	----
Bowl, 10½″ Ruffled Edge	14.00	----	Saucer	1.00	7.00
Butter Dish & Cover	15.00	----	Snack Plate	25.00	----
Cup	4.50	12.00	Tumbler	9.00	----

CORONATION, "BANDED FINE RIB", "SAXON"
(pink, crystal, royal ruby)
HOCKING GLASS COMPANY, 1936-1940

	Pink	Red		Pink	Red
Bowl, 4¼" Berry	3.00	5.00	Plate, 6" Sherbet	1.25	----
Bowl, 6½" Nappy	3.50	8.00	Plate, 8½" Luncheon	3.50	6.00
Bowl, 8" Large Berry	7.00	12.00	Saucer	1.25	----
Cup	3.50	4.50	Sherbet	3.50	----
Pitcher, 7¾", 68 oz.	150.00	----	Tumbler, 5", 10 oz. Footed	12.00	----

CREMAX
(cremax, decal decorations)
MacBETH-EVANS DIVISION OF CORNING GLASS WORKS,
Late 1930s - Early 1940s

	Ivory	Ivory Decorated		Ivory	Ivory Decorated
Bowl, 5¾" Cereal	2.50	6.00	Plate, 9¾" Dinner	3.50	6.00
Bowl, 9" Vegetable	5.50	9.00	Plate, 11½" Sandwich . . .	4.00	7.50
Creamer	3.00	6.00	Saucer	1.50	1.50
Cup	3.00	3.50	Sugar, Open	3.00	6.00
Plate, 6¼" Bread & Butter	1.50	2.50			

CUBE, "CUBIST"
(pink, green, crystal)
JEANNETTE GLASS COMPANY, 1929-1933

	Pink	Green		Pink	Green
Bowl, 4½" Dessert	4.00	5.00	Plate, 6" Sherbet	1.50	2.50
Bowl, 4½" Deep	4.50	----	Plate, 8" Luncheon	3.00	4.50
Bowl, 6½" Salad	7.00	12.00	Powder Jar & Cover, 3 Legs	13.00	17.50
Butter Dish & Cover	40.00	45.00	Salt & Pepper, Pr.	25.00	27.50
Candy Jar & Cover, 6½" .	21.50	25.00	Saucer	1.50	2.00
Coaster, 3¼"	3.50	4.50	Sherbet, Footed	4.50	6.00
Creamer, 2"	2.00	----	Sugar, 2"	2.00	----
Creamer, 3"	4.50	6.00	Sugar, 3"	3.50	6.00
Cup	4.50	7.00	Sugar/Candy Cover	6.50	8.50
Pitcher, 8¾", 45 oz.	140.00	150.00	Tumbler, 4", 9 oz.	35.00	42.50

"DAISY," Number 620
(crystal, 1933; amber, 1940; dark green and milk glass, 1960s)
INDIANA GLASS COMPANY

	Crystal	Amber		Crystal	Amber
Bowl, 4½" Berry	4.00	7.00	Plate, 9⅜" Dinner	3.50	6.00
Bowl, 4½" Cream Soup	3.00	7.50	Plate, 10⅜" Grill	4.00	9.50
Bowl, 6" Cereal	10.00	20.00	Plate, 11½" Cake or		
Bowl, 7⅜"Deep Berry	6.00	10.00	Sandwich	5.00	9.00
Bowl, 9⅜" Deep Berry	9.00	24.00	Platter, 10¾"	5.00	10.00
Bowl, 10" Oval Vegetable	6.00	12.50	Relish Dish, 3 Part, 8⅜"	9.00	20.00
Creamer, Footed	4.50	6.50	Saucer	1.00	1.50
Cup	2.50	4.50	Sherbet, Footed	4.00	7.00
Plate, 6" Sherbet	1.00	2.00	Sugar, Footed	4.00	6.50
Plate, 7⅜" Salad	2.00	5.50	Tumbler, 9 oz. Footed	5.00	14.00
Plate, 8⅜" Luncheon	2.00	5.50	Tumbler, 12 oz. Footed	15.00	27.50

DIAMOND QUILTED, "FLAT DIAMOND"
(pink, blue, green, crystal, black)
IMPERIAL GLASS COMPANY, Late 1920s - Early 1930s

	Green	Blue		Green	Blue
Bowl, 4¾" Cream Soup ..	6.50	15.00	Pitcher, 64 oz...........	40.00	----
Bowl, 5" Cereal	4.00	8.00	Plate, 6" Sherbet	2.00	3.00
Bowl, 5½" One Handle...	5.50	8.50	Plate, 7" Salad	4.00	5.50
Bowl, 7" Crimped Edge...	5.50	10.00	Plate, 8" Luncheon	4.00	9.50
Bowl, Rolled Edge Console	15.00	30.00	Plate, 14" Sandwich	10.00	----
Cake Salver, Tall 10"			Punch Bowl & Stand.....	350.00	----
Diameter	40.00	----	Sandwich Server, Center		
Candlesticks (2 styles) Pr..	8.50	22.50	Handle	17.50	35.00
Candy Jar & Cover, Footed	40.00	----	Saucer	1.50	3.50
Compote & Cover, 11½"..	55.00	----	Sherbet	3.50	8.00
Creamer	6.00	9.50	Sugar	5.50	9.00
Cup	5.00	8.00	Tumbler, 9 oz. Water	6.00	----
Goblet, 1 oz. Cordial	8.00	----	Tumbler, 12 oz. Iced Tea .	7.00	----
Goblet, 2 oz. Wine	8.00	----	Tumbler, 6 oz. Footed ...	5.00	----
Goblet, 3 oz. Wine	8.00	----	Tumbler, 9 oz. Footed ...	8.50	----
Goblet, 6", 9 oz. Champagne	7.50	----	Tumbler, 12 oz. Footed ..	12.50	----
Ice Bucket..............	37.50	55.00	Whiskey, 1½ oz.	6.00	----
Mayonnaise Set: Ladle,					
Plate, 3 Footed Dish ...	27.50	----			

DIANA
(pink, amber, crystal)
FEDERAL GLASS COMPANY, 1937-1941

	Pink	Amber		Pink	Amber
Ash Tray, 3½"	3.00	----	Plate, 5½" Child's	3.00	----
Bowl, 5" Cereal.........	3.50	----	Plate, 6" Bread & Butter .	1.50	1.50
Bowl, 5½" Cream Soup ..	5.50	6.00	Plate, 9½" Dinner.......	6.00	6.50
Bowl, 9" Salad	6.50	6.50	Plate, 11¾" Sandwich ...	6.00	6.50
Bowl, 11" Console Fruit ..	6.50	8.00	Platter, 12" Oval	7.00	8.00
Bowl, 12" Scalloped Edge	7.50	8.00	Salt & Pepper, Pr........	45.00	80.00
Candy Jar & Cover, Round	20.00	25.00	Saucer	1.50	1.50
Coaster, 3½"	3.00	----	Sherbet	5.50	8.00
Creamer, Oval	4.50	4.50	Sugar, Open, Oval	4.50	4.50
Cup	4.00	4.00	Tumbler, 4⅛", 9 oz......	15.00	18.00
Cup, Demitasse, 2 oz. & 4½" Saucer Set	18.00	----			

DOGWOOD, "APPLE BLOSSOM," "WILD ROSE"
(pink, green,)
MacBETH-EVANS COMPANY, 1929-1932

	Pink	Green
Bowl, 5½" Cereal	16.00	19.00
Bowl, 8½" Berry	37.50	75.00
Bowl, 10¼" Fruit	210.00	110.00
Cake Plate, 11" Heavy Solid Foot	175.00	----
Cake Plate, 13" Heavy Solid Foot	70.00	60.00
Creamer, 2½" Thin	13.00	40.00
Creamer, 3¼" Thick	13.50	----
Cup, Thin or Thick	10.00	20.00
Pitcher, 8", 80 oz. Decorated	125.00	435.00
Pitcher, 8", 80 oz (American Sweetheart Style)	450.00	----
Plate, 6" Bread & Butter .	4.50	5.50
Plate, 8" Luncheon	4.75	5.00
Plate, 9¼" Dinner	17.50	----

	Pink	Green
Plate, 10½" Grill AOP or Border Design Only	13.00	13.50
Plate, 12" Salver	20.00	----
Platter, 12" Oval (Rare) . .	265.00	----
Saucer	4.50	5.00
Sherbet, Low Footed	20.00	60.00
Sugar, 2½" Thin	11.00	37.50
Sugar, 3¼" Thick	10.50	----
Tumbler, 3½", 5 oz. Decorated	210.00	----
Tumbler, 4", 10 oz. Decorated	25.00	60.00
Tumbler, 4¾", 11 oz. Decorated	30.00	65.00
Tumbler, 5", 12 oz. Decorated	35.00	75.00

DORIC
(pink, green)
JEANNETTE GLASS COMPANY, 1935-1938

	Pink	Green		Pink	Green
Bowl, 4½" Berry	5.00	5.50	Plate, 7" Salad	12.50	12.50
Bowl, 5" Cream Soup	----	175.00	Plate, 9" Dinner	7.50	10.00
Bowl, 5½" Cereal	22.00	30.00	Plate, 9" Grill	9.00	12.50
Bowl, 8¼" Large Berry	9.50	12.50	Platter, 12" Oval	12.50	14.00
Bowl, 9" Two Handled	9.50	10.00	Relish Tray, 4" x 4"	4.50	7.50
Bowl, 9" Oval Vegetable	12.00	17.00	Relish Tray, 4" x 8"	6.50	9.50
Butter Dish & Cover	55.00	68.00	Salt & Pepper, Pr.	25.00	27.50
Cake Plate, 10" Three Legs	12.50	12.50	Saucer	2.00	2.50
Candy Dish & Cover, 8"	25.00	27.50	Sherbet, Footed	7.50	9.50
Candy Dish, Three Part	4.50	5.50	Sugar	9.00	10.00
Coaster, 3"	10.00	12.00	Sugar Cover	10.00	17.50
Creamer, 4"	7.50	8.50	Tray, 10" Handled	7.50	9.50
Cup	5.50	6.50	Tray, 8" x 8" Serving	7.50	10.00
Pitcher, 6", 36 oz. Flat	25.00	30.00	Tumbler, 4½", 9 oz. Flat	30.00	50.00
Pitcher, 7½", 48 oz. Footed	300.00	625.00	Tumbler, 4", 10 oz. Ftd.	25.00	50.00
Plate, 6" Sherbet	2.50	3.00	Tumbler, 5", 12 oz. Ftd.	40.00	60.00

DORIC and PANSY
(pink, crystal, ultramarine)
JEANNETTE GLASS COMPANY, 1937-1938

	Pink	Ultra-marine
Bowl 4½" Berry	6.50	10.00
Bowl, 8" Large Berry	17.50	60.00
Bowl, 9" Handled	12.00	25.00
Butter Dish & Cover	----	400.00
Cup	----	15.00
Creamer	----	105.00
Plate, 6" Sherbet	5.00	7.00
Plate, 7" Salad	----	25.00
Plate, 9" Dinner	----	18.00
Salt & Pepper, Pr.	----	300.00
Saucer	----	3.00
Sugar, Open	----	100.00
Tray, 10" Handled	----	15.00

	Pink	Ultra-marine
Tumbler, 4½", 9 oz.	----	37.50

DORIC AND PANSY
"PRETTY POLLY PARTY DISHES"

	Pink	Ultra-marine
Cup	20.00	25.00
Saucer	3.00	4.00
Plate	5.00	7.00
Creamer	22.50	30.00
Sugar	22.50	30.00
14 Piece Set	150.00	190.00

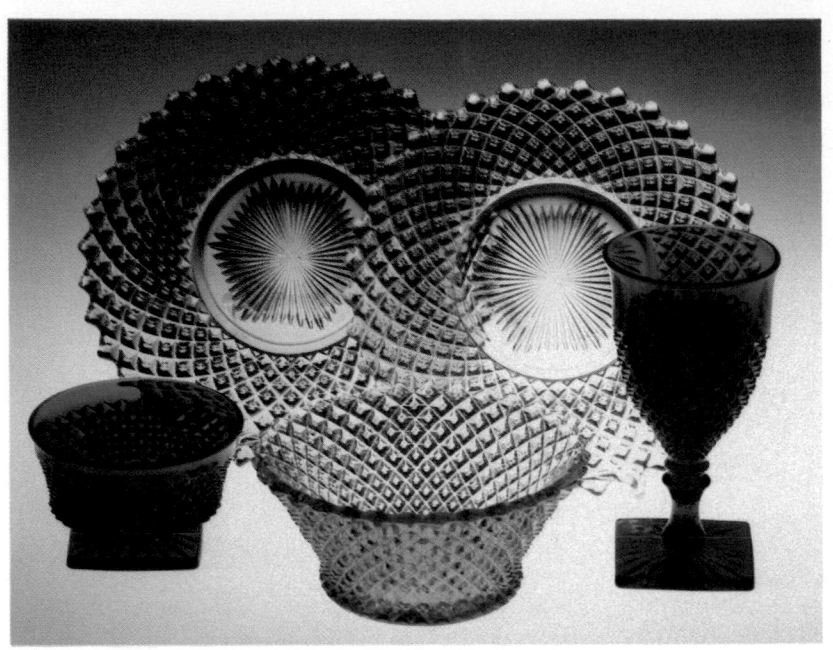

ENGLISH HOBNAIL
(crystal, pink, amber, turquoise, cobalt, green)
WESTMORELAND GLASS COMPANY, 1920s-1970s

	Pink or Green		Pink or Green
Ash Tray, Several Shapes	18.50	Cigarette Box	25.00
Bowls, 4½", 5" Square &		Cologne Bottle..........	25.00
Round...............	9.50	Creamer, Footed or Flat ..	20.00
Bowl, Cream Soup	13.50	Cup	12.00
Bowls, 6", Several Styles .	10.00	Decanter, 20 oz. w/Stopper	85.00
Bowls, 8", Several Styles .	22.00	Demitasse Cup & Saucer .	25.00
Bowls, 8", Footed & Two		Egg Cup	32.50
Handled	45.00	Goblet, 1 oz. Cordial.....	22.50
Bowls, 11" & 12" Nappies	37.50	Goblet, 2 oz. Wine	15.00
Bowls, Relish, Oval, 8" & 9"	17.50	Goblet, 3 oz. Cocktail	15.00
Bowl, Relish, Oval, 12" ..	18.00	Goblet, 5 oz. Claret......	18.00
Candlesticks, 3½", Pr....	30.00	Goblet, 6¼", 8 oz.	20.00
Candlesticks, 8½", Pr....	45.00	Grapefruit, 6½", Flange Rim	14.00
Candy Dish, ½ lb., Cone		Lamp, 6¼" Electric	50.00
Shaped..............	40.00	Lamp, 9¼"	100.00
Candy Dish & Cover, Three		Marmalade & Cover	30.00
Feet	65.00	Pitcher, 23 oz...........	135.00
Celery Dish, 9"	20.00	Pitcher, 39 oz...........	155.00
Celery Dish, 12"	25.00	Pitcher, 60 oz...........	190.00

	Pink or Green		Pink or Green
Pitcher, ½ Gal. Straight Sides	200.00	Saucer	3.50
Plate, 5½" & 6½" Sherbet	3.50	Sherbet	12.50
Plate, 7¼" Pie	4.00	Sugar, Footed or Flat	20.00
Plate, 8" Round or Square	7.50	Tumbler, 3¾", 5 oz. or 8 oz.	13.00
Plate, 10" Dinner	23.00	Tumbler, 4", 10 oz. Iced Tea	15.00
Salt & Pepper, Pr., Round or Square Bases	67.50	Tumbler, 5", 12 oz. Iced Tea	20.00
		Tumbler, 7 oz. Footed ...	13.50
Salt Dip, 2" Footed & w/Place Card Holder ...	20.00	Tumbler, 9 oz. Footed ...	15.00
		Tumbler, 12½ oz. Footed .	20.00
		Whiskey, 1½ & 3 oz.	22.00

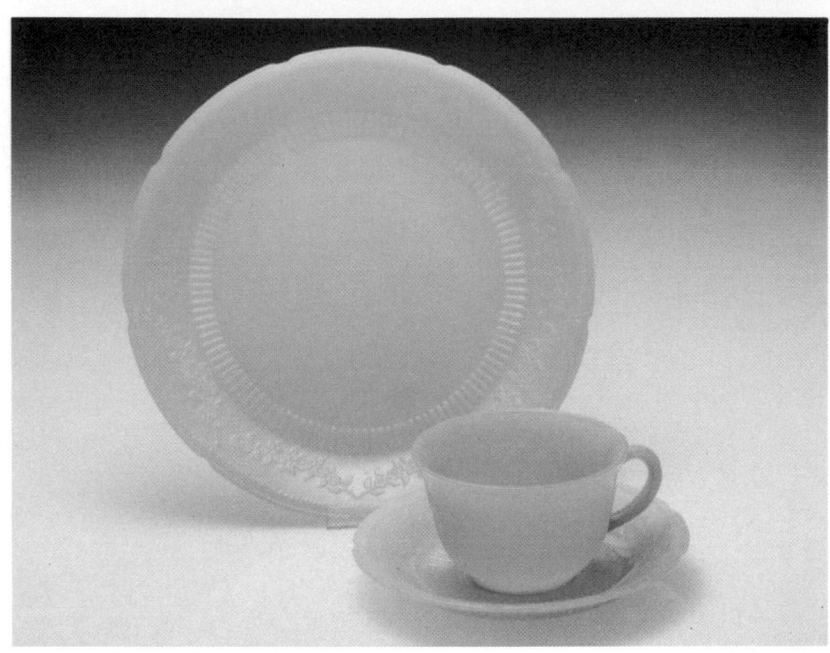

FIRE-KING DINNERWARE, "ALICE"
ANCHOR HOCKING COMPANY, 1940s

	Jade-ite		Jade-ite
*Cup	1.25	***Saucer	.50
**Plate, 8½"	5.00		

*Add $1.50 for White w/Trim
**Add $.25 for White w/Trim
***Add $.50 for White w/Trim

FIRE KING DINNERWARE, "JANE RAY"
ANCHOR HOCKING COMPANY, 1945-1960s

	Jade-ite		Jade-ite
Bowl, 4⅞" Dessert	1.50	Plate, 7¾" Salad	1.50
Bowl, 5⅞" Oatmeal	2.00	Plate, 9⅛" Dinner	2.50
Bowl, 7⅝" Soup	3.00	Platter, 12"	5.00
Bowl, 8¼" Vegetable	4.00	Saucer	.50
Cup	1.25	Sugar	1.50
Creamer	2.25	Sugar & Cover	2.50

FIRE KING DINNERWARE, "SQUARE"
ANCHOR HOCKING GLASS CORPORATION, 1940s-1960s

	All Colors		All Colors
Bowl, 4¾" Dessert	3.00	Plate, 8⅜" Luncheon	3.00
Bowl, 7⅜" Salad	5.25	Plate, 9¼", Dinner	3.75
Cup	2.25	Saucer	.50

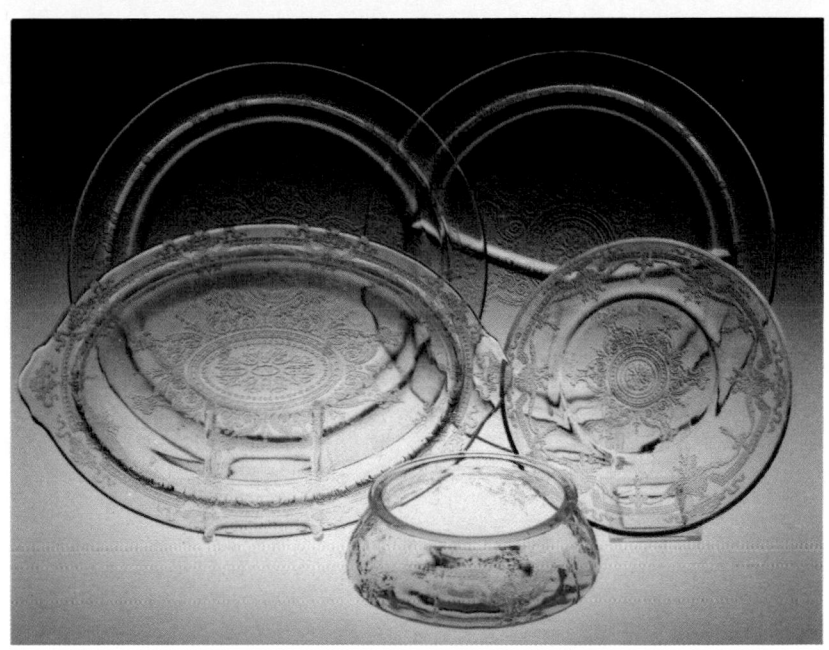

FIRE KING DINNERWARE, "PHILBE"
(blue, pink, green and crystal)
ANCHOR HOCKING GLASS COMPANY, 1937-1938

	All Colors		All Colors
Bowl, 5½" Cereal	30.00	Plate, 10½" Salver	35.00
Bowl, 7¼" Salad	40.00	Plate, 10½" Grill	30.00
Bowl, 10" Oval Vegetable	45.00	Plate, 11⅝" Salver	30.00
Candy Jar, 4" Low w/Cover	225.00	Platter, 12" Closed Handles	75.00
Cookie Jar w/Cover	325.00	Saucer, 6" (same as	
Creamer, 3¼" Footed . . .	65.00	sherbet)	30.00
Cup	90.00	Sugar, 3¼" Footed	65.00
Goblet, 7¼" Thin, 9 oz. . .	150.00	Tumbler, 4", 9 oz. Flat Water	100.00
Pitcher, 6" Juice, 36 oz. . .	500.00	Tumbler, 3½" Footed Juice	125.00
Pitcher, 8½", 54 oz.	600.00	Tumbler, 5¼" Footed, 10	
Plate, 6" Sherbet	30.00	oz.	50.00
Plate, 8" Luncheon	25.00	Tumbler, 6½" Footed, 15	
Plate, 10" Heavy Sandwich	27.50	oz. Iced Tea	45.00

FIRE-KING OVEN GLASS
(blue, 1940s; crystal, 1950s)
ANCHOR HOCKING GLASS COMPANY

	Blue		Blue
Baker, 1 Pt., Rd. or Sq. . . .	3.50	Loaf Pan, 9⅛″ Deep	20.00
Baker, 1 Qt.	4.50	Nurser, 4 oz.	12.00
Baker, 1½ Qt.	8.50	Nurser, 8 oz.	15.00
Baker, 2 Qt.	10.00	Pie Plate, 4⅜″ Individual .	9.00
Cake Pan (deep), 8¾″ . . .	14.00	Pie Plate, 5⅜″ Deep Dish	10.00
Casserole, 1 Pt., Knob		Pie Plate, 8⅜″	7.00
Handle Cover	10.00	Pie Plate, 9″	8.00
Casserole, 1 Qt., Knob		Pie Plate, 9⅝″	9.00
Handle Cover	10.00	Pie Plate, 10⅜″ Juice	
Casserole, 1½ Qt., Knob		Saver	50.00
Handle Cover	12.50	Perculator Top, 2⅛″	3.50
Casserole, 2 Qt., Knob		Refrigerator Jar & Cover,	
Handle Cover	15.00	4½″ x 5″	7.50
Casserole, 1 Qt., Pie Plate		Refrigerator Jar & Cover,	
Cover	12.50	5⅛″ x 9⅛″	15.00
Casserole, 1½ Qt., Pie Plate		Roaster, 8¾″	30.00
Cover	15.00	Roaster, 10⅜″	50.00
Casserole, 2 Qt., Pie Plate		Table Server, Tab Handles	
Cover	18.00	(Hot Plate)	10.00
Casserole, 10 oz., Tab		Utility Bowl, 6⅞″	8.00
Handle Cover	12.00	Utility Bowl, 8⅜″	10.00
Coffee Mug, 7 oz.	17.50	Utility Bowl, 10⅛″	15.00
Cup, 8 oz. Measuring	10.00	Utility Pan, 10½″,	
Custard Cup, 5 oz.	2.50	Rectangular	15.00
Custard Cup, 6 oz., 2 Styles	3.00	Utility Pan, 8⅛″ x 12½″ .	12.50

FIRE KING OVEN WARE TURQUOISE BLUE
(turquoise blue)
ANCHOR HOCKING GLASS CORPORATION, 1950s

	Blue		Blue
Bowl, 4½″ Berry	3.00	Creamer	4.00
Bowl, 5″ Cereal	4.50	Cup	2.00
Bowl, 6⅝″ Soup/Salad	7.00	Mug, 8 oz.	5.00
Bowl, 8″ Vegetable	9.00	Plate, 6⅛″	2.50
Bowl, Tear, Mixing, 1 Pt.	4.00	Plate, 7″	4.00
Bowl, Tear, Mixing, 1 Qt.	5.00	Plate, 9″	4.00
Bowl, Tear, Mixing, 2 Qt.	6.00	Plate, 9″ w/Cup Indent	4.00
Bowl, Tear, Mixing, 3 Qt.	7.00	Plate, 10″	8.00
Bowl, Round, Mixing, 1 Qt.	4.00	Relish, 3 Part	6.00
Bowl, Round, Mixing, 2 Qt.	5.00	Saucer	.50
Bowl, Round, Mixing, 3 Qt.	6.00	Sugar	3.75
Bowl, Round, Mixing, 4 Qt.	7.00		

FIRE-KING OVEN WARE "SWIRL"
(blue, pink, white w/gold trim, ivory w/trims, jade-ite)
ANCHOR HOCKING GLASS CORPORATION, 1955-1960s

	Jade-ite	Others		Jade-ite	Others
Bowl, Berry, 4⅞"	2.25	3.00	Platter, 12"	7.50	10.00
Creamer	2.25	3.50	Saucer	.50	.75
Cup	2.00	2.50	Sugar	1.50	2.00
Plate, 6⅞" Salad	1.50	1.75	Sugar Cover	2.00	2.50
Plate, Dinner, 9⅛"	2.75	4.00			

FLORAGOLD, "LOUISA"
(iridescent, shell pink, crystal)
JEANNETTE GLASS COMPANY, 1950s

	Irides-cent		Irides-cent
Bowl, 4½" Square	4.50	Cup	4.50
Bowl, 5½" Cereal Round .	20.00	Pitcher, 64 oz...........	26.00
Bowl, 5½" Ruffled Fruit ..	4.50	Plate, 5¾" Sherbet......	6.50
Bowl, 8½" Square	12.00	Plate, 8½" Dinner.......	18.00
Bowl, 9½" Salad, Deep ..	27.50	Plate or Tray, 13½"	12.50
Bowl, 9½" Ruffled	6.50	Indent on 13½" Plate ..	27.50
Bowl, 12" Ruffled, Large		Platter, 11¼"	14.00
Fruit	6.50	Salt & Pepper, Plastic Tops	35.00
Butter Dish & Cover, ¼ lb.		Saucer (same as sherbet	
Oblong	17.50	plate)	6.50
Butter Dish & Cover, Round	35.00	Sherbet, Low Footed	8.00
Ⅹ Candlesticks, Double		Sugar	5.00
Branch, Pr...........	32.50	Sugar Lid	7.50
Candy or Cheese Dish &		Tumbler, 10 oz. Footed ..	12.50
Cover, 6¾"	35.00	Tumbler, 11 oz. Footed ..	12.50
Candy, 5¼" Long, 4 Feet	4.50	Tumbler, 15 oz., Footed ..	45.00
Coaster—Ash Tray, 4" ...	4.50	Vase or Celery	155.00
Creamer	6.25		

FLORAL "POINSETTA"
(pink, green, delphite)
JEANNETTE GLASS COMPANY, 1931-1935

	Pink	Green
Bowl, 4" Berry	11.00	12.00
Bowl, 5½" Cream Soup	600.00	600.00
Bowl, 7½" Salad	10.00	12.00
Bowl, 8" Covered Vegetable	25.00	32.50
Bowl, 9" Oval Vegetable	11.00	13.00
Butter Dish & Cover	70.00	75.00
✳ Candlesticks, 4", Pr.	50.00	70.00
Candy Jar & Cover	28.00	33.00
Creamer, Flat	9.00	10.00
Coaster, 3¼"	7.50	8.00
Compote, 9"	500.00	600.00
Cup	7.50	8.50
Ice Tub, Oval, 3½" High	550.00	600.00
Lamp	225.00	225.00
Pitcher, 5½", 23 or 24 oz. Flat	----	475.00
Pitcher, 8", 32 oz. Footed Cone	20.00	25.00
Pitcher, 10¼", 48 oz. Lemonade	145.00	175.00
Plate, 6" Sherbet	3.50	4.00
Plate, 8" Salad	7.00	7.50
Plate, 9" Dinner	11.00	12.50
Plate, 9" Grill	----	150.00

	Pink	Green
Platter, 10¾" Oval	11.00	12.50
Refrigerator Dish & Cover, 5" Square	----	50.00
Relish Dish, Oval, Two Part	10.00	11.00
Salt & Pepper, Pr., 4" Footed	35.00	40.00
Salt & Pepper, 6" Flat (pink)	40.00	----
Saucer	6.00	6.50
Sherbet	10.00	12.00
Sugar	7.50	8.50
Sugar/Candy Cover	9.50	12.50
Tray, 6" Square, Closed Handles	10.00	12.00
Tumbler, 4", 5 oz. Footed Juice	12.00	15.00
Tumbler, 4¾", 7 oz. Footed Water	12.00	15.00
Tumbler, 5¼", 9 oz. Footed Lemonade	32.00	34.00
Vase, 3 Legged Rose Bowl	----	400.00
Vase, 3 Legged Flared (Also in Crystal)	----	400.00
Vase, 6⅞" Tall (8 sided)	----	375.00

FLORAL and DIAMOND BAND
(crystal, pink, green)
U.S. GLASS COMPANY, 1927-1931

	Pink	Green		Pink	Green
Bowl, 4½" Berry	5.00	6.00	Plate, 8" Luncheon	17.50	16.00
Bowl, 5¾" Nappy, Handled	7.00	7.00	Sherbet	5.00	6.00
Bowl, 8" Large Berry	9.50	10.00	Sugar, Small	7.00	8.00
Butter Dish & Cover	80.00	85.00	Sugar, 5¼"	10.00	10.00
Compote, 5½" Tall	9.50	11.00	Sugar Lid	30.00	30.00
Creamer, Small	7.00	8.00	Tumbler, 4" Water	12.00	14.00
Creamer, 4¾"	12.00	15.00	Tumbler, 5" Iced Tea	16.00	20.00
Pitcher, 8", 42 oz	70.00	80.00			

FLORENTINE NO. 1, "POPPY NO. 1"
(pink, green, crystal, yellow, cobalt)
HAZEL ATLAS GLASS COMPANY, 1934-1936

	Green	Yellow		Green	Yellow
Ash Tray, 5½"	19.00	25.00	Plate, 10" Dinner	10.00	17.50
Bowl, 5" Berry	8.00	12.00	Plate, 10" Grill	8.00	11.00
Bowl, 6" Cereal	15.00	17.00	Platter, 11½" Oval	10.00	16.00
Bowl, 8½" Large Berry	17.50	22.00	Salt & Pepper, Footed	30.00	45.00
Bowl, 9½" Oval Vegetable			Saucer	2.00	3.50
& Cover	35.00	40.00	Sherbet, 3 oz. Footed	6.00	8.50
Butter Dish & Cover	100.00	145.00	Sugar	8.00	10.00
Coaster/Ash Tray, 3¾"	14.00	16.00	Sugar Cover	11.50	15.00
Creamer	7.50	10.00	Sugar, Ruffled	25.00	----
Creamer, Ruffled	25.00	----	Tumbler, 3¾", 5 oz. Footed		
Cup	6.00	8.00	Juice	10.00	17.50
Pitcher, 6½", 36 oz. Footed	32.50	40.00	Tumbler, 4¾", 10 oz.		
Pitcher, 7½", 54 oz. Flat Ice			Footed Water	17.00	15.00
Lip or None	40.00	150.00	Tumbler, 5¼", 12 oz.		
Plate, 6" Sherbet	3.00	4.50	Footed Iced Tea	20.00	25.00
Plate, 8½" Salad	6.00	9.50			

FLORENTINE NO. 2, "POPPY NO. 2"
(pink, green, yellow, crystal, cobalt blue)
HAZEL ATLAS GLASS COMPANY, 1932-1935

	Green	Yellow		Green	Yellow
Bowl, 4½" Berry	9.00	13.50	Plate, 6" Sherbet	2.50	4.00
Bowl, 4¾" Cream Soup	10.00	15.00	Plate, 6¼" w/Indent for		
Bowl, 5¼"	25.00	30.00	Custard	13.50	22.50
Bowl, 6" Cereal	20.00	27.00	Plate, 8½" Salad	6.00	7.00
Bowl, 8" Large Berry	15.00	20.00	Plate, 10" Dinner	10.00	12.00
Bowl, 9" Oval Vegetable &			Plate, 10¼" Grill	6.50	8.00
Cover	35.00	45.00	Platter, 11" Oval	11.00	13.50
Butter Dish & Cover	85.00	125.00	Platter, 11½" for Gravy Boat	----	32.50
✗ Candlesticks, 2¾", Pr.	35.00	45.00	Relish Dish, 10", 3 Part or		
Candy Dish & Cover	85.00	135.00	Plain	13.00	17.50
Coaster, 3¼"	10.00	17.00	Salt & Pepper, Pr.	35.00	40.00
Coaster/Ash Tray, 3¾"	13.00	18.00	Saucer	2.50	3.00
Coaster/Ash Tray, 5½"	15.00	28.00	Sherbet, Footed	7.00	8.00
Compote, 3½" Ruffled	15.00	----	Sugar	6.50	8.50
Creamer	6.50	8.50	Sugar Cover	10.00	15.00
Cup	6.00	7.00	Tumbler, 3½", 5 oz. Juice	9.00	17.50
Custard Cup or Jello	45.00	65.00	Tumbler, 4", 9 oz. Water	10.00	16.00
Gravy Boat	----	35.00	Tumbler, 5", 12 oz. Iced Tea	22.00	32.50
Pitcher, 7½", 28 oz. Cone			Tumbler, 3¼", 5 oz. Footed	10.00	11.00
Footed	20.00	22.50	Tumbler, 4", 5 oz. Footed	10.00	11.00
Pitcher, 7½", 54 oz.	40.00	142.50	Tumbler, 4½", 9 oz. Footed	17.50	22.50
Pitcher, 8", 76 oz.	77.50	300.00	Vase or Parfait, 6"	25.00	45.00

FLOWER GARDEN WITH BUTTERFLIES, "BUTTERFLIES AND ROSES"
(pink, green, blue-green, canary yellow, amber, black)
U.S. GLASS COMPANY, Late 1920s

	All Colors		All Colors
Ash Tray, Match-Pack		Cup	50.00
Holders	155.00	Plate, 8", Two Styles	16.00
Bowl, Rolled Edge Console	75.00	Powder Jar, Footed	75.00
Candlesticks, 4", Pr.	45.00	Powder Jar, Flat	50.00
Candlesticks, 8", Pr.	85.00	Sandwich Server, Center	
Candy Dish & Cover, 7½"	100.00	Handle	50.00
Candy Dish, Open, 6"	25.00	Saucer	20.00
Cheese & Cracker Set (4"		Sugar, Open	65.00
Compote, 10" Plate)	50.00	Tray, 5½" x 10" Oval	47.50
Cologne Bottle, 7½", Tall		Tray, Rectangular,	
Footed	150.00	11¾" x 7¾"	60.00
Console Bowl, 10" Footed	77.50	Vase, 7" (black)	120.00
Creamer	65.00	Vase, 10"	110.00

FOREST GREEN
(dark green glass)
ANCHOR HOCKING, 1950s-1967

	Green		Green
Ash Tray	3.00	Pitcher, 3 Qt. Round	20.00
Bowl, 4¾" Dessert	4.00	Platter, Rectangular	18.00
Bowl, 6" Soup	8.00	Saucer	1.00
Bowl, 7⅜" Salad	7.50	Sugar, Flat	4.50
Creamer, Flat	4.50	Tumbler, 5 oz.	2.00
Cup	2.50	Tumbler, 10 oz.	4.00
Plate, 6⅝" Salad	2.00	Vase, 4" Ivy	3.00
Plate, 8⅜" Luncheon	4.00	Vase, 6⅜"	3.50
Plate, 10" Dinner	8.50	Vase, 9"	5.00

"FORTUNE"
(pink, crystal)
HOCKING GLASS COMPANY, 1937-1938

	Pink		Pink
Bowl, 4" Berry	3.00	Cup	3.00
Bowl, 4½" Dessert	3.50	Plate, 6" Sherbet	2.00
Bowl, 4½" Handled	3.50	Plate, 8" Luncheon	6.00
Bowl, 5¼" Rolled Edge	4.50	Saucer	2.00
Bowl, 7¾" Salad or Large		Tumbler, 3½", 5 oz. Juice	3.50
Berry	8.00	Tumbler, 4", 9 oz. Water	4.50
Candy Dish & Cover, Flat	15.00		

"FRUITS"
(pink, green, crystal)
HAZEL ATLAS AND OTHER GLASS COMPANIES, 1931-1953

	Pink	Green	Pink		Green
Bowl, 5" Cereal	11.00	12.50			
Bowl, 8" Berry	30.00	35.00	Sherbet	5.50	6.00
Cup	----	4.50	Tumbler, 3½" Juice	7.00	8.00
Pitcher, 7" Flat Bottom	----	45.00	Tumbler, 4" (One Fruit)	7.50	8.00
Plate, 8" Luncheon	4.00	4.00	Tumbler, 4" (Combination of		
Saucer	2.00	2.50	Fruits)	8.00	11.00
			Tumbler, 5", 12 oz	25.00	40.00

GEORGIAN, "LOVEBIRDS"
(green, crystal)
FEDERAL GLASS COMPANY, 1931-1936

	Green
Bowl, 4½" Berry	5.50
Bowl, 5¾" Cereal	14.50
Bowl, 6½" Deep	50.00
Bowl, 7½" Large Berry . .	42.50
Bowl, 9" Oval Vegetable .	47.50
Butter Dish & Cover	67.50
Cold Cuts Server, 18½" Wood w/Seven 5" Openings for 5" Coasters . . .	500.00
Creamer, 3" Footed	8.50
Creamer, 4" Footed	10.00
Cup	7.50
Hot Plate, 5" Center Design	32.50
Plate, 6" Sherbet	3.00

	Green
Plate, 8" Luncheon	5.50
Plate, 9¼" Dinner	18.00
Plate, 9¼" Center Design Only	16.00
Platter, 11½" Closed Handled	47.50
Saucer	2.00
Sherbet	8.00
Sugar, 3" Footed	7.50
Sugar, 4" Footed	8.50
Sugar Cover, 3"	22.50
Sugar Cover, 4"	60.00
Tumbler, 4", 9 oz. Flat . . .	37.50
Tumbler, 5¼", 12 oz. Flat	70.00

HARP
(crystal and crystal with gold rims)
JEANNETTE GLASS COMPANY, 1954-1957

	Crystal		Crystal
Ash Tray/Coaster	3.50	Plate, 7″	4.50
Coaster	2.00	Saucer	2.00
Cup	5.50	Tray, Rectangular	20.00
Cake Stand, 9″	16.50	Vase, 6″..............	10.00

HERITAGE
(crystal, pink, blue, green)
FEDERAL GLASS COMPANY, Late 1930s-1960s

	Crystal		Crystal
Bowl, 5″ Berry	4.50	Plate, 8″ Luncheon	5.00
Bowl, 8½″ Large Berry	20.00	Plate, 9¼″ Dinner	7.00
Bowl, 10½″ Fruit	12.00	Plate, 12″ Sandwich	8.50
Cup	4.00	Saucer	2.00
Creamer, Footed	16.00	Sugar, Open, Footed	11.00

HEX OPTIC, "HONEYCOMB"
(pink, green)
JEANNETTE GLASS COMPANY, 1928-1932

	Pink or Green		Pink or Green
Bowl, 4¼" Berry, Ruffled .	2.50	Plate, 8" Luncheon	4.50
Bowl, 7½" Large Berry . .	5.00	Platter, 11" Round	7.00
Butter Dish & Cover,		Refrigerator Dish, 4" x 4"	7.00
Rectangular, 1 lb. Size .	55.00	Salt & Pepper, Pr.	20.00
Bucket Reamer	40.00	Saucer	1.50
Creamer, 2 Style Handles	4.00	Sugar, 2 Styles of Handles	4.00
Cup, 2 Style Handles	4.00	Sugar Shaker	90.00
Ice Bucket, Metal Handle .	12.50	Sherbet, 5 oz. Footed	3.50
Pitcher, 5", 32 oz. Sunflower		Tumbler, 3¾", 9 oz.	4.00
Motif in Bottom	15.00	Tumbler, 5¾", Footed . . .	5.00
Pitcher, 9", 48 oz. Footed	30.00	Tumbler, 7" Footed	8.00
Plate, 6" Sherbet	1.50	Whiskey, 2", 1 oz.	5.00

HOBNAIL
(crystal, pink)
HOCKING GLASS COMPANY, 1934-1936

	Crystal		Crystal
Bowl, 5½" Cereal	2.50	Sherbet	2.00
Cup	3.00	Sugar, Footed	3.00
Creamer, Footed	3.00	Tumbler, 5 oz. Juice	3.00
Decanter & Stopper, 32 oz.	17.50	Tumbler, 9 oz., 10 oz. Water	4.50
Goblet, 10 oz. Water	4.50	Tumbler, 15 oz. Iced Tea .	5.00
Goblet, 13 oz. Ice Tea	5.00	Tumbler, 3 oz. Footed Wine	5.00
Pitcher, 18 oz. Milk	13.00	Tumbler, 5 oz. Footed	
Pitcher, 67 oz.	20.00	Cordial	5.00
Plate, 6" Sherbet	1.00	Whiskey, 1½ oz.	4.00
Saucer	1.00		

HOLIDAY, "BUTTON and BOWS"
(pink, iridescent)
JEANNETTE GLASS COMPANY, 1947-1949

	Pink		Pink
Bowl, 5⅛″ Berry	7.00	Plate, 6″ Sherbet	3.00
Bowl, 7¾″ Soup	27.50	Plate, 9″ Dinner	9.50
Bowl, 8½″ Large Berry . .	14.50	Plate, 13¾″ Chop	67.50
Bowl, 9½″ Oval Vegetable	12.50	Platter, 11⅜″ Oval	10.00
Bowl, 10¾″ Console	75.00	Sandwich Tray, 10½″	9.00
Butter Dish & Cover	30.00	Saucer, Two Styles	3.00
Cake Plate, 10½″, 3 Legged	65.00	Sherbet	5.00
X Candlesticks, 3″, Pr.	60.00	Sugar	5.00
Creamer, Footed	6.50	Sugar Cover	8.50
Cup, Two Sizes	5.00	Tumbler, 4″, 10 oz. Flat . .	15.00
Pitcher, 4¾″, 16 oz. Milk .	47.50	Tumbler, 4″ Footed	27.50
Pitcher, 6¾″, 52 oz.	25.00	Tumbler, 6″ Footed	67.50

HOMESPUN, "FINE RIB"
(pink, crystal)
JEANNETTE GLASS COMPANY, 1939-1940

	Pink or Crystal
Bowl, 4½" Closed Handles	4.50
Bowl, 5" Cereal	12.50
Bowl, 8¼" Large Berry	11.00
Butter Dish & Cover	40.00
Coaster/Ash Tray	4.50
Creamer, Footed	6.50
Cup	4.50
Plate, 6" Sherbet	2.50
Plate, 9¼" Dinner	8.50
Platter, 13" Closed Handles	8.50
Saucer	2.00
Sherbet, Low Flat	6.50
Sugar, Footed	6.50
Tumbler, 4", 9 oz. Water	10.00
Tumbler, 5¼", 13 oz. Iced Tea	20.00

	Pink or Crystal
Tumbler, 4", 5 oz. Footed	5.00
Tumbler, 6¼", 9 oz. Footed	17.50
Tumbler, 6½", 15 oz. Footed	20.00

HOMESPUN'S CHILD'S TEA SET

	Pink or Crystal
Cup	22.50
Saucer	6.00
Plate	9.00
Tea Pot	25.00
Tea Pot Cover	35.00
Set 14 Pieces	210.00

INDIANA CUSTARD, "FLOWER and LEAF BAND"
(ivory or custard, early 1930s, white, 1950s)
INDIANA GLASS COMPANY

	Ivory		Ivory
Bowl, 4⅞" Berry	7.00	Plate, 7½" Salad	8.50
Bowl, 5¾" Cereal	15.00	Plate, 8⅞" Luncheon	8.50
Bowl, 7½" Flat Soup	25.00	Plate, 9¾" Dinner	13.50
Bowl, 8¾" Large Berry . .	22.00	Platter, 11½" Oval	22.50
Bowl, 9½" Oval Vegetable	20.00	Saucer	5.00
Butter Dish & Cover	52.50	Sherbet	70.00
Cup	32.00	Sugar	7.50
Creamer	12.50	Sugar Cover	15.00
Plate, 5¾" Bread & Butter	4.50		

IRIS, "IRIS and HERRINGBONE"
(crystal, iridescent)
JEANNETTE GLASS COMPANY, 1928-1932; 1950; 1970

	Crystal	Irides-cent		Crystal	Irides-cent
Bowl, 4½" Berry, Beaded	28.00	6.50	Goblet, 4½" Wine	13.00	----
Bowl, 5" Sauce	5.50	5.00	Goblet, 5¾", 4 oz.	16.00	----
Bowl, 5" Cereal	35.00	----	Goblet, 5¾", 8 oz.	15.00	40.00
Bowl, 7½" Soup	80.00	30.00	Pitcher, 9½" Footed	20.00	27.50
Bowl, 8" Large Berry,			Plate, 5½" Sherbet	7.50	6.00
Beaded	55.00	10.00	Plate, 8" Luncheon	35.00	----
Bowl, 9½" Salad	8.50	8.00	Plate, 9" Dinner	30.00	20.00
Bowl, 11" Fruit, Ruffled	8.50	6.00	Plate, 11¾" Sandwich	12.00	11.00
Bowl, 11" Fruit, Straight	33.00	----	Saucer	5.00	4.00
Butter Dish & Cover	27.50	30.00	Sherbet, 2½" Footed	16.00	10.00
Candlesticks, Pr.	17.50	22.50	Sherbet, 4" Footed	12.50	----
Candy Jar & Cover	72.50	----	Sugar	6.00	6.50
Coaster	32.50	----	Sugar Cover	6.50	7.00
Creamer, Footed	7.00	8.00	Tumbler, 4" Flat	50.00	----
Cup	8.50	7.50	Tumbler, 6" Footed	12.00	12.00
Demitasse Cup	20.00	65.00	Tumbler, 6½" Footed	15.00	----
Demitasse Saucer	60.00	75.00	Vase, 9"	15.00	14.00
Goblet, 4" Wine	----	17.00			

JUBILEE
(topaz)
LANCASTER GLASS COMPANY, Early 1930s

	Topaz		Topaz
Bowl, 9″ Fruit, Handled ..	50.00	Plate, 7″ Salad	6.50
✗ Candlesticks, Pr.........	75.00	Plate, 8¾″ Luncheon	9.00
Cheese & Cracker Set ...	65.00	Plate, 13″ Sandwich	25.00
Creamer..............	17.50	Saucer	3.00
Cup	10.00	Sherbet, 4¾″	25.00
Goblet, 5″, 6 oz........	35.00	Sugar	16.00
Goblet, 6″, 10 oz.......	25.00	Tray, 11″ Cake, 2 Handles	30.00
Goblet, 6⅛″, 12½ oz. ...	65.00	Tray, Sandwich Center	
Mayonnaise, w/Plate &		Handle	45.00
Ladle...............	125.00		

LACED EDGE, "KATY BLUE"
(blue, with opalescent edge; green with opalescent edge)
IMPERIAL GLASS COMPANY, Early 1930s

	Blue/Green		Blue/Green
Bowl, 4½" Fruit	15.00	Plate, 10" Dinner	27.50
Bowl, 7" Soup	20.00	Plate, 12" Luncheon (per	
Bowl, 9" Vegetable	45.00	catalogue description)	35.00
Bowl, 11" Divided Oval	40.00	Platter, 13"	55.00
Bowl, 11" Oval	45.00	Saucer	7.50
Cup	17.50	Sugar	19.00
Creamer	20.00	Tidbit, w/8" & 10" plates	55.00
Mayonnaise, 3 Pc.	65.00	Tumbler, 9 oz.	27.50
Plate, 6½" Bread & Butter	9.50	Vase, 5½"	40.00
Plate, 8" Salad	15.00		

LACE EDGE, "OPEN LACE"
(pink, crystal)
HOCKING GLASS COMPANY, 1935-1938

	Pink		Pink
Bowl, 6⅜" Cereal	12.50	Plate, 7¼" Salad	14.00
Bowl, 7¾" Salad	15.00	Plate, 8¾" Luncheon	12.50
Bowl, 9½" Plain or Ribbed	14.00	Plate, 10½" Dinner.	19.00
Bowl, 10½", 3 Legs	135.00	Plate, 10½" Grill.	13.00
Butter Dish or Bon Bon		Plate, 13", 4-Part Solid Lace	18.50
w/Cover	45.00	Platter, 12¾"	19.00
𝕏 Candlesticks, Pr.	135.00	Platter, 12¾", 5-Part	19.00
Candy Jar & Cover, Ribbed	35.00	Relish Dish, 7½" Deep,	
Compote, 7"	17.50	3-Part	45.00
Compote & Cover, Footed	30.00	Saucer	7.50
Cookie Jar & Cover.	45.00	Sherbet, Footed	50.00
Creamer.	16.00	Sugar	15.00
Cup	16.50	Tumbler, 4½", 9 oz. Flat .	10.00
Fish Bowl, 1 gal. 8 oz.		Tumbler, 5", 10½ oz.	
(Crystal Only)	17.50	Footed	47.50
Flower Bowl, Crystal Frog	17.50	Vase, 7".	245.00

LAKE COMO
(white with blue decoration)
ANCHOR HOCKING GLASS COMPANY, 1934-1937

Bowl, 6″ Cereal	12.00	Plate, Dinner, 9¼″	12.50
Bowl, Flat Soup	55.00	Platter, 11″	22.50
Bowl, Vegetable, 9¾″	20.00	Salt & Pepper, Pr.	25.00
Creamer, Footed	12.50	Saucer	5.00
Cup	12.00	Sugar, Footed	11.00
Plate, Salad, 7¼″	7.50		

LAUREL
(French ivory, jade green, white opal and poudre blue)
McKEE GLASS COMPANY, 1930s

	Ivory	Green		Ivory	Green
Bowl, 5″ Berry	5.00	4.00	Salt & Pepper	35.00	45.00
Bowl, 6″ Cereal	6.00	5.00	Saucer	2.50	2.00
Bowl, 6″ Three Legs	9.00	10.00	Sherbet	9.50	7.50
Bowl, 9″ Large Berry	15.00	12.00	Sugar, Short	7.50	7.00
Bowl, 9¾″ Oval Vegetable	15.00	15.00	Sugar, Tall	10.00	8.50
Bowl, 10½″ Three Legs	27.50	25.00	Tumbler, 4½″, 9 oz. Flat	25.00	35.00
Bowl, 11″	27.50	25.00	Tumbler, 5″, 12 oz. Flat	35.00	----
✗ Candlesticks, 4″ Pr.	25.00	25.00			
Cheese Dish & Cover	50.00	40.00			
Creamer, Short	9.00	8.00	**CHILDREN'S LAUREL TEA SET**		
Creamer, Tall	10.00	9.00			
Cup	6.00	6.00	Creamer	20.00	32.50
Plate, 6″ Sherbet	3.50	2.50	Cup	15.00	20.00
Plate, 7½″ Salad	8.00	8.00	Plate	7.50	12.50
Plate, 9⅛″ Dinner	7.50	7.50	Saucer	5.50	7.50
Plate, 9⅛″ Grill	7.50	7.00	Sugar	20.00	32.50
Platter, 10¾″ Oval	20.00	15.00	14 Piece Set	150.00	225.00

LINCOLN INN
(amethyst, cobalt, black, red, green, pink, crystal, jade, opaque, green)
FENTON GLASS COMPANY, Late 1920s

	Blue, Red	Other Colors		Blue, Red	Other Colors
Ash Tray	15.00	10.00	Nut Dish, Footed	15.00	10.00
Bon Bon, Handled, Sq.	13.00	10.00	Pitcher, 7¼", 46 oz.	750.00	500.00
Bon Bon, Handled, Oval	13.00	10.00	Plate, 6"	6.00	3.00
Bowl, 5" Fruit	9.50	7.00	Plate, 8"	10.00	6.00
Bowl, 6" Cereal	10.00	7.00	Plate, 9¼"	12.50	10.00
Bowl, 6" Crimped	11.00	7.00	Plate, 12"	17.50	10.00
Bowl, Handled, Olive	12.00	7.00	Salt & Pepper, Pr.	150.00	125.00
Bowl, Finger	15.00	10.00	Saucer	3.00	2.00
Bowl, 9¼" Footed	25.00	15.00	Sherbet, 4¾"	15.00	10.00
Bowl, 10½" Footed	35.00	25.00	Sugar	16.50	12.00
Candy Dish, Footed, Oval	18.00	10.00	Tumbler, 4 oz. Flat Juice	15.00	7.50
Comport	20.00	12.00	Tumbler, 5 oz. Footed	15.00	8.50
Creamer	17.50	12.00	Tumbler, 7 oz. Footed	15.00	9.00
Cup	14.00	7.50	Tumbler, 9 oz. Footed	15.00	12.00
Goblet, Water	20.00	12.00	Tumbler, 12 oz. Footed	25.00	15.00
Goblet, Wine	25.00	15.00	Vase, 12" Footed	95.00	65.00

LORAIN, "BASKET," "NO. 615"
(green, yellow, crystal)
INDIANA GLASS COMPANY, 1929-1932

	Green	Yellow		Green	Yellow
Bowl, 6" Cereal	27.50	45.00	Plate, 8⅜" Luncheon	13.00	22.00
Bowl, 7¼" Salad	32.50	45.00	Plate, 10¼" Dinner	30.00	42.50
Bowl, 8" Deep Berry	65.00	110.00	Platter, 11½"	19.00	30.00
Bowl, 9¾" Oval Vegetable	27.50	37.50	Relish, 8", 4-Part	13.50	22.50
Creamer, Footed	12.00	16.00	Saucer	3.50	4.50
Cup	8.50	11.50	Sherbet, Footed	15.00	25.00
Plate, 5½" Sherbet	5.50	7.50	Sugar, Footed	10.00	16.00
Plate, 7¾" Salad	8.00	12.00	Tumbler, 4¾", 9 oz. Footed	15.00	20.00

MADRID
(See Reproduction Section, Page 142)
(green, pink, amber, crystal, "Madonna" blue)
FEDERAL GLASS COMPANY, 1932-1939

	Amber	Green		Amber	Green
Ash Tray, 6" Square	150.00	100.00	Plate, 6" Sherbet	2.50	3.50
Bowl, 4¾" Cream Soup . .	10.00	----	Plate, 7½" Salad	8.00	7.50
Bowl, 5" Sauce	5.00	6.00	Plate, 8⅞" Luncheon	6.00	7.50
Bowl, 7" Soup	9.50	11.00	Plate, 10½" Dinner	27.50	30.00
Bowl, 8" Salad	11.50	15.00	Plate, 10½" Grill	8.50	14.00
Bowl, 9⅜" Large Berry . .	14.50	----	Plate, 10¼" Relish	10.00	15.00
Bowl, 9½" Deep Salad . .	22.00	----	Plate, 11¼" Cake Round .	10.00	----
Bowl, 10" Oval Vegetable	12.50	13.50	Platter, 11½" Oval	10.50	13.00
Bowl, 11" Low Console . .	11.50	----	Salt/Pepper, 3½" Footed .	57.50	77.50
Butter Dish & Cover	55.00	70.00	Salt/Pepper, 3½" Flat . . .	37.50	60.00
Candlesticks, 2¼", Pr. . . .	16.00	----	Saucer	2.50	3.50
Cookie Jar & Cover	32.50	----	Sherbet, Two Styles	7.00	7.50
Creamer, Footed	6.00	8.50	Sugar	6.50	7.50
Cup	5.00	6.00	Sugar Cover	27.50	32.50
Gravy Boat & Platter	1000.00	----	Tumbler, 3⅞", 5 oz.	12.50	30.00
Hot Dish Coaster	27.50	27.50	Tumbler, 4¼", 9 oz.	12.00	20.00
Hot Dish Coaster w/Indent	30.00	27.50	Tumbler, 5½", 12 oz., 2		
Jam Dish, 7"	18.00	15.00	Styles	17.00	27.50
Jello Mold, 2⅛" High	9.00	----	Tumbler, 4", 5 oz. Footed	20.00	32.50
Pitcher, 5½", 36 oz. Juice	30.00	----	Tumbler, 5½", 10 oz.		
Pitcher, 8", 60 oz. Square	37.50	110.00	Footed	20.00	30.00
Pitcher, 8½", 80 oz.	50.00	185.00	Wooden Lazy Susan, 7 Hot		
Pitcher, 8½", 80 oz. Ice Lip	50.00	185.00	Dish Coasters	500.00	----

MANHATTAN, "HORIZONTAL RIBBED"
(pink, crystal, green)
ANCHOR HOCKING GLASS COMPANY, 1939-1941

	Crystal	Pink		Crystal	Pink
Ash Tray, 4" Round	8.00	----	Relish Tray, 14", 4-Part . .	15.00	15.00
Ash Tray, 4½" Square . . .	15.00	----	Relish Tray, 14", 5-Part . .	13.00	15.00
Bowl, 4½" Sauce	5.00	6.00	Relish Tray Insert	3.50	4.50
Bowl, 5⅜" Berry w/Handles	11.00	12.00	Pitcher, 42 oz.	15.00	30.00
Bowl, 7½" Large Berry . .	8.50	8.50	Pitcher, 80 oz. Tilted.	22.00	35.00
Bowl, 8" Closed Handles .	13.00	18.00	Plate, 6" Sherbet	4.00	25.00
Bowl, 9" Salad	12.00	15.00	Plate, 8½" Salad	7.50	----
Bowl, 9½" Fruit	17.50	20.00	Plate, 10¼" Dinner.	10.00	50.00
Candlesticks, 4½" (Square)			Plate, 14" Sandwich	10.00	----
Pr.	12.00	----	Salt/Pepper, 2" Pr. (Square)	18.00	30.00
Candy Dish, 3 Legs	----	7.50	Saucer (Same as 6" Plate)	4.00	25.00
Candy Dish & Lid	25.00	----	Sherbet	6.50	6.00
Coaster, 3½"	5.50	----	Sugar, Oval	7.00	6.00
Compote, 5¾"	15.00	15.00	Tumbler, 10 oz. Footed . .	10.00	10.00
Creamer, Oval	7.00	7.00	Vase, 8".	11.50	----
Cup	11.00	95.00	Wine, 3½"	5.00	----

MAYFAIR FEDERAL
(crystal, amber, green)
FEDERAL GLASS COMPANY, 1934

	Amber	Green		Amber	Green
Bowl, 5″ Sauce	5.00	7.00	Plate, 9½″ Dinner	10.00	10.00
Bowl, 5″ Cream Soup	13.50	13.50	Plate, 9½″ Grill	9.00	9.00
Bowl, 6″ Cereal	14.00	16.00	Platter, 12″ Oval	20.00	20.00
Bowl, 10″ Oval Vegetable	15.00	18.00	Saucer	2.50	2.50
Creamer, Footed	10.00	13.00	Sugar, Footed	10.00	12.50
Cup	5.50	6.50	Tumbler, 4½″, 9 oz.	17.50	20.00
Plate, 6¾″ Salad	4.50	6.00			

MAYFAIR, "OPEN ROSE"
(See Reproduction Section, Page 145)
(pink, green, blue, yellow, crystal)
HOCKING GLASS COMPANY, 1931-1937

	Pink	Blue		Pink	Blue
Bowl, 5" Cream Soup....	34.00	----	Goblet, 4" Cocktail, 3½ oz.	57.50	----
Bowl, 5½" Cereal........	16.00	36.00	Goblet, 4½" Wine, 3 oz. .	57.50	----
Bowl, 7" Vegetable......	17.50	35.00	Goblet, 5¾" Water, 9 oz..	45.00	----
Bowl, 9", 3⅛" High, 3 Leg			Goblet, 7¼" Thin, 9 oz...	115.00	115.00
Console	3250.00	----	Pitcher, 6", 37 oz........	32.00	92.50
Bowl, 9½" Oval Vegetable	19.00	40.00	Pitcher, 8", 60 oz........	35.00	110.00
Bowl, 10" Vegetable.....	16.00	40.00	Pitcher, 8½", 80 oz......	62.50	130.00
Bowl, 10" Same Covered.	70.00	80.00	Plate, 5¾" (often		
Bowl, 11¾" Low Flat	35.00	45.00	substituted as saucer)..	9.00	13.50
Bowl, 12" Deep Scalloped			Plate, 6½" Round Sherbet	9.00	----
Fruit	37.50	52.50	Plate, 6½" Round, Off		
Butter Dish & Cover or 7"			Center Indent	19.50	18.00
Covered Vegetable	42.50	220.00	Plate, 8½" Luncheon	16.00	27.50
Cake Plate, 10" Footed ..	18.00	40.00	Plate, 9½" Dinner.......	36.00	45.00
Candy Dish & Cover	37.50	145.00	Plate, 9½" Grill.........	25.00	25.00
Celery Dish, 10"	22.00	30.00	Plate, 12" Cake w/Handles	26.00	42.50
Celery Dish 10", Divided .	125.00	35.00	Platter, 12" Oval Open		
Cookie Jar & Lid	32.50	160.00	Handles	15.00	35.00
Creamer, Footed	15.00	47.50	Relish, 8⅜", 4-Part or Non-		
Cup	13.00	35.00	Partitioned	20.00	35.00
Decanter & Stopper, 32 oz.	110.00	----	Salt & Pepper, Pr., Flat ..	42.50	190.00

	Pink	Blue		Pink	Blue
Salt & Pepper, Pr., Footed	3500.00	----	Tumbler, 4¾", 11 oz. Water	110.00	85.00
Sandwich Server/Center			Tumbler, 5¼", 13½ oz.		
Handle	27.50	45.00	Iced Tea	33.00	115.00
Saucer (Cup Ring)	21.00	----	Tumbler, 3¼", 3 oz. Footed		
Saucer (See 5¾" Plate) . .			Juice	55.00	----
Sherbet, 2¼" Flat	110.00	65.00	Tumbler, 5¼", 10 oz.		
Sherbet, 3" Footed	12.00	----	Footed	27.50	87.50
Sherbet, 4¾" Footed	55.00	50.00	Tumbler, 6½", 15 oz.		
Sugar, Footed	17.50	47.50	Footed Iced Tea	27.50	110.00
Sugar Lid	1350.00	----	Vase, (Sweet Pea)	105.00	70.00
Tumbler, 3½", 5 oz. Juice	30.00	75.00	Whiskey, 2¼", 1½ oz. . . .	50.00	----
Tumbler, 4¼", 9 oz. Water	22.00	65.00			

MISS AMERICA
(See Reproduction Section, Page 148)
(pink, green, crystal, red)
HOCKING GLASS COMPANY, 1933-1937

	Crystal	Pink		Crystal	Pink
Bowl, 6¼" Berry	6.00	12.50	Plate, 5¾" Sherbet	3.00	5.00
Bowl, 8" Curved in at Top	30.00	50.00	Plate, 8½" Salad	5.00	14.00
Bowl, 8¾" Straight Deep			Plate, 10½" Dinner	10.00	17.00
Fruit	22.50	42.50	Plate, 10¼" Grill	7.50	15.00
Bowl, 10" Oval Vegetable	10.00	17.00	Platter, 12" Oval	10.00	17.50
Butter Dish & Cover	190.00	425.00	Relish, 8¾", 4-Part	7.50	15.00
Cake Plate, 12" Footed	16.50	27.50	Relish, 11¾" Round		
Candy Jar & Cover, 11½"	45.00	95.00	Divided	15.00	400.00
Celery Dish, 10½" Oblong	7.50	15.00	Salt & Pepper, Pr.	22.50	42.50
Coaster, 5¾"	12.50	18.50	Saucer	2.50	4.00
Compote, 5"	11.00	17.00	Sherbet	6.50	10.00
Creamer, Footed	6.50	12.50	Sugar	6.00	12.50
Cup	7.50	16.00	Tumbler, 4", 5 oz. Juice	14.00	37.50
Goblet, 3¾", 3 oz. Wine	16.00	50.00	Tumbler, 4½", 10 oz. Water	12.00	20.00
Goblet, 4¾", 5 oz. Juice	20.00	62.50	Tumbler, 5¾", 14 oz. Iced		
Goblet, 5½", 10 oz. Water	17.50	35.00	Tea	22.00	47.50
Pitcher, 8", 65 oz.	40.00	85.00			
Pitcher, 8½", 65 oz w/Ice					
Lip	57.50	97.50			

MODERNTONE, "WEDDING BAND"
(blue, amethyst, platonite fired-on colors)
HAZEL ATLAS GLASS COMPANY, 1934-1942

	Cobalt	Amethyst		Cobalt	Amethyst
Ash Tray, 7¾" Match Holder in Center	110.00	----	Plate, 6¾" Salad	7.00	6.00
Bowl, 4¾" Cream Soup	13.00	12.00	Plate, 7¾" Luncheon	6.50	6.00
Bowl, 5" Berry	15.00	12.00	Plate, 8⅞" Dinner	10.00	7.50
Bowl, 5" Cream Soup Ruffled	20.00	17.50	Plate, 10½" Sandwich	25.00	17.50
Bowl, 6½" Cereal	42.50	35.00	Platter, 11" Oval	25.00	20.00
Bowl, 7½" Soup	55.00	45.00	Platter, 12" Oval	35.00	27.50
Bowl, 8¾" Large Berry	27.50	22.00	Salt & Pepper, Pr.	27.50	27.50
Butter Dish w/Metal Cover	65.00	----	Saucer	2.00	2.00
Cheese Dish, 7" w/Metal Lid	200.00	----	Sherbet	8.50	7.50
Creamer	7.50	6.00	Sugar	7.50	6.50
Cup	7.50	5.00	Sugar Lid in Metal	22.50	----
Cup (Handle-less) Custard	10.50	9.50	Tumbler, 5 oz.	20.00	15.00
Plate, 5¾" Sherbet	3.75	3.00	Tumbler, 9 oz.	17.00	17.50
			Tumbler, 12 oz.	55.00	45.00
			Whiskey, 1½ oz.	15.00	----

MOONDROPS
(amber, pink, green, cobalt blue, ice blue, red, amethyst, crystal, dark green, light green, jadite, smoke, black)
NEW MARTINSVILLE, 1932-1940s

	Red, Blue	Others
Ash Tray	30.00	14.00
Bowl, 5¼″ Berry	10.00	5.00
Bowl, 6¾″ Soup	12.00	10.00
Bowl, 7½″ Pickle	17.00	13.00
Bowl, 8⅜″ Footed Concave Top	30.00	19.00
Bowl, 8½″ Three Footed Divided Relish	22.00	16.00
Bowl, 9½″ Three Legged, Ruffled	30.00	20.00
Bowl, 9¾″ Oval Vegetable	25.00	20.00
Bowl, 9¾″ Covered Casserole	100.00	75.00
Bowl, 9¾″ Two Handled Oval	45.00	30.00
Bowl, 11½″ Celery, Boat Shaped	25.00	20.00
Bowl, 12″ Three Footed, Round Console	40.00	25.00
Bowl, 13″ Console w/"wings"	62.50	35.00
Butter Dish & Cover	360.00	200.00
Candles, 2″ Ruffled, Pr.	25.00	20.00
Candles, 4½″ Sherbet Style, Pr.	22.50	16.00
Candlesticks, 5″ "wings," Pr.	65.00	40.00
Candlesticks, 5¼″ Triple Light, Pr.	75.00	45.00
Candlesticks, 8½″ Metal Stem, Pr.	32.50	25.00
Candy Dish, 8″ Ruffled	25.00	15.00
Cocktail Shaker with or without handle, metal top	30.00	20.00
Compote, 4″	17.50	10.00
Compote, 11½″	40.00	25.00
Creamer, 2¾″ Miniature	10.00	8.00
Creamer, 3¾″, Regular	12.00	7.50

	Red, Blue	Others		Red, Blue	Others
Cup	10.00	7.50	Plate, 8½" Luncheon	11.00	8.00
Decanter, Small, 7¾"	50.00	35.00	Plate, 9½" Dinner	15.00	12.00
Decanter, Medium, 8½"	60.00	40.00	Plate, 14" Round Sandwich	25.00	14.00
Decanter, Large, 11¼"	70.00	45.00	Plate, 14" Two Handled Sandwich	30.00	20.00
Decanter, "rocket", 10¼"	195.00	100.00			
Goblet, 2⅞" , ¾ oz. Liquor	22.00	18.00	Platter, 12" Oval	20.00	15.00
Goblet, 4", 4 oz. Wine	15.00	10.00	Saucer	3.50	3.00
Goblet, 4¼" "rocket" Wine	45.00	25.00	Sherbet, 2⅝"	10.00	7.50
Goblet, 4¾", 5 oz.	18.00	12.00	Sherbet, 4½"	20.00	12.50
Goblet, 5⅛" Metal Stem Wine	12.00	8.50	Sugar, 2¾"	9.00	7.00
Goblet, 5½" Metal Stem Wine	13.50	8.50	Sugar, 4"	11.00	7.00
			Tumbler, 2¾" Shot, 2 oz.	10.00	6.50
Goblet, 6¼" Metal Stem Water, 9 oz.	17.50	13.50	Tumbler, 2¾" Handled Shot, 2 oz.	12.50	7.50
Mug, 5⅛", 12 oz.	30.00	20.00	Tumbler, 3¾" Footed Juice, 3 oz.	11.50	7.50
Perfume Bottle, "rocket"	125.00	75.00			
Pitcher, Small, 6⅞", 22 oz.	135.00	75.00	Tumbler, 3⅝", 5 oz.	10.00	6.00
Pitcher, Medium, 8⅛", 32 oz.	150.00	100.00	Tumbler, 4⅜", 7 oz.	11.00	7.50
			Tumbler, 4⅜", 8 oz.	12.00	8.50
Pitcher, Large w/Lip, 8", 50 oz.	155.00	110.00	Tumbler, 4⅞" Handled, 9 oz.	20.00	12.50
Pitcher, Large, No Lip, 8⅛", 53 oz.	150.00	115.00	Tumbler, 4⅞", 9 oz.	13.50	10.00
			Tumbler, 5⅛", 12 oz.	20.00	11.50
Plate, 5⅞" Bread & Butter	3.50	2.50	Tray, 7½" for Miniature Sugar/Creamer	25.00	15.00
Plate, 6⅛" Sherbet	5.00	2.50	Vase, 7¾" Flat, Ruffled Top	50.00	35.00
Plate, 6" Round, Off-Center Indent for Sherbet	9.00	7.00	Vase, 9¼" "rocket" style	135.00	75.00
Plate, 7⅛" Salad	9.00	7.00			

MOONSTONE
(crystal with opalescent hobnails)
ANCHOR HOCKING GLASS COMPANY, 1941-1946

	Opal-escent		Opal-escent
Bowl, 5½" Berry	9.00	Goblet, 10 oz.	15.00
Bowl, 5½" Crimped Dessert	6.00	Heart Bonbon, One Handle	8.50
Bowl, 6½" Crimped		Plate, 6¼" Sherbet	2.50
Handled	7.00	Plate, 8" Luncheon	8.50
Bowl, 7¾" Flat	9.00	Plate, 10" Sandwich	16.00
Bowl, 7¾" Divided Relish	7.50	Puff Box & Cover, 4¾"	
Bowl, 9½" Crimped	12.50	Round	16.00
Bowl, Cloverleaf	8.50	Saucer (Same as Sherbet	
Candleholder, Pr.	15.00	Plate)	2.50
Candy Jar & Cover, 6"	17.50	Sherbet, Footed	6.00
Cigarette Jar & Cover	15.00	Sugar, Footed	6.00
Creamer	6.00	Vase, 5½" Bud	8.50
Cup	6.00		

MOROCCAN AMETHYST
(amethyst)
HAZEL WARE, DIVISION OF CONTINENTAL CAN, 1960s

	Amethyst		Amethyst
Ash Tray, 6⅞″ Triangular	5.00	Plate, 12″ Sandwich	6.00
Bowl, 4¾″ Fruit	3.50	Saucer	.75
Bowl, 5¾″ Cereal	4.50	Tumbler, Juice, 2½″, 4 oz.	3.50
Candy w/Lid	17.50	Tumbler, Old Fashion, 3¼″,	
Cocktail Shaker, 32 oz. . .	15.00	8 oz.	6.00
Cup	3.00	Tumbler, Water, 4½″, 11 oz.	5.50
Plate, 7¼″ Salad	2.00	Tumbler, Iced Tea, 16 oz.	8.00
Plate, 9⅜″ Dinner	4.00	Vase, 9″, Ruffled	27.50

MT. PLEASANT, "DOUBLE SHIELD"
(black, cobalt blue, green, pink)
L.E. SMITH COMPANY, 1920s-1934

	Black Amethyst, Cobalt		Black Amethyst, Cobalt
Bonbon, Rolled Up Handles, 7″	17.50	Cup	8.50
Bowl, 4″ Opening Rose	20.00	Leaf, 8″	11.00
Bowl, 4″ Square Footed Fruit	15.00	Mayonnaise, 5½″, 3 Footed	20.00
Bowl, 6″ Two Handled Square	12.50	Mint, 6″ Center Handle	15.00
Bowl, 7″, 3 Footed, Rolled Out Edge	16.50	Plate, 7″, 2 Handled, Scalloped	10.00
Bowl, 8″ Scalloped, 2 Handled	20.00	Plate, 8″ Scalloped or Square	11.00
Bowl, 8″ Square, 2 Handled	20.00	Plate, 8″, 2 Handled	13.50
Bowl, 9″ Scalloped, 1¾″ Deep, Footed	25.00	Plate, 8¼″ Sq. w/Indent for Cup	13.00
Bowl, 9¼″ Sq. Footed Fruit	22.50	Plate, 9″ Grill	8.50
Bowl, 10″ Scalloped Fruit	30.00	Plate, 10½″ Cake, 2 Handled	20.00
Bowl, 10″, 2 Handled, Turned Up Edge	25.00	Plate, 12″, 2 Handled	25.00
Candlesticks, Single, Pr.	20.00	Salt & Pepper, 2 Styles	32.50
Candlesticks, Double, Pr.	32.00	Sandwich Server, Center Handled	30.00
Creamer	12.50	Sherbet	12.50
Cup (Waffle-like Crystal)	----	Sugar	12.50
		Vase, 7¼″	20.00

NEW CENTURY, and incorrectly, "LYDIA RAY"
(pink, green, crystal, amethyst, cobalt)
HAZEL ATLAS GLASS COMPANY, 1930-1935

	Green		Green
Ash Tray/Coaster, 5⅜" . . .	25.00	Plate, 8½" Salad	6.00
Bowl, 4½" Berry	5.00	Plate, 10" Dinner	10.00
Bowl, 4¾" Cream Soup . .	9.00	Plate, 10" Grill	8.00
Bowl, 8" Large Berry	12.00	Platter, 11" Oval	11.00
Bowl, 9" Covered Casserole	45.00	Salt & Pepper, Pr.	27.50
Butter Dish & Cover	47.50	Saucer	2.00
Cup	5.00	Sherbet, 3"	6.00
Creamer	6.00	Sugar	5.00
Decanter & Stopper	40.00	Sugar Cover	9.00
Goblet, 2½ oz. Wine	14.00	Tumbler, 3½", 5 oz.	8.00
Goblet, 3¼ oz. Cocktail . .	14.00	Tumbler, 4⅛", 9 oz.	10.00
Pitcher, 7¾", 60 oz. with or		Tumbler, 5", 10 oz.	10.00
without Ice Lip	27.50	Tumbler, 5¼", 12 oz.	15.00
Pitcher, 8", 80 oz. with or		Tumbler, 4", 5 oz. Footed	10.00
without Ice Lip	30.00	Tumbler, 4⅞", 9 oz. Footed	12.50
Plate, 6" Sherbet	2.25	Whiskey, 2½", 1½ oz. . . .	12.00
Plate, 7⅛" Breakfast	5.50		

NEWPORT, "HAIRPIN"
(cobalt blue, amethyst, "Platonite" white and fired on colors)
HAZEL ATLAS GLASS COMPANY, 1936-1940

	Cobalt	Amethyst		Cobalt	Amethyst
Bowl, 4¼" Berry	10.00	9.00	Plate, 11½" Sandwich	25.00	22.00
Bowl, 4¾" Cream Soup	13.00	12.00	Platter, 11¾" Oval	27.50	23.00
Bowl, 5¼" Cereal	22.00	16.00	Salt & Pepper	35.00	32.50
Bowl, 8¼" Large Berry	30.00	25.00	Saucer	2.50	2.50
Cup	7.50	6.50	Sherbet	9.00	8.50
Creamer	10.00	9.00	Sugar	10.00	9.00
Plate, 6" Sherbet	3.50	3.50	Tumbler, 4½", 9 oz.	22.50	20.00
Plate, 8½" Luncheon	7.50	7.50			

NORMANDIE, "BOUQUET and LATTICE"
(iridescent, amber, pink)
FEDERAL GLASS COMPANY, 1933-1940

	Amber	Pink		Amber	Pink
Bowl, 5" Berry	4.00	5.00	Plate, 11" Grill	10.00	12.50
Bowl, 6½" Cereal	9.00	12.00	Platter, 11¾"	11.00	17.00
Bowl, 8½" Large Berry	11.00	15.00	Salt & Pepper, Pr.	37.50	55.00
Bowl, 10" Oval Vegetable	12.00	23.00	Saucer	1.50	2.00
Creamer, Footed	6.00	8.50	Sherbet	5.00	6.50
Cup	5.50	6.50	Sugar	5.00	6.00
Pitcher, 8", 80 oz.	50.00	85.00	Sugar Lid	65.00	100.00
Plate, 6" Sherbet	2.00	2.00	Tumbler, 4", 5 oz. Juice	12.50	32.50
Plate, 8" Salad	6.50	8.50	Tumbler, 4¼", 9 oz. Water	11.00	30.00
Plate, 9¼" Luncheon	5.00	9.50	Tumbler, 5", 12 oz. Iced Tea	17.00	45.00
Plate, 11" Dinner	17.50	60.00			

NO. 610, "PYRAMID"
(green, pink, yellow, crystal)   (black, 1974-75 by Tiara)
INDIANA GLASS COMPANY, 1928-1932

	Pink	Yellow		Pink	Yellow
Bowl, 4¾" Berry	14.50	25.00	Pitcher	200.00	395.00
Bowl, 8½" Master Berry	20.00	45.00	Relish Tray, 4-Part, Handled	30.00	50.00
Bowl, 9½" Oval	25.00	45.00	Sugar	17.50	25.00
Bowl, 9½" Pickle	25.00	45.00	Tray for Creamer & Sugar	17.50	40.00
Creamer	18.00	25.00	Tumbler, 8 oz. Footed	20.00	42.50
Ice Tub	65.00	175.00	Tumbler, 11 oz. Footed	35.00	55.00
Ice Tub & Lid	----	600.00			

NO. 612 "HORSESHOE"
(green, yellow, crystal)
INDIANA GLASS COMPANY, 1930-1933

	Green	Yellow
Bowl, 4½" Berry	16.00	15.00
Bowl, 6½" Cereal	15.00	16.50
Bowl, 7½" Salad	14.00	16.00
Bowl, 8½" Vegetable	17.00	22.50
Bowl, 9½" Large Berry . .	25.00	27.00
Bowl, 10½" Oval Vegetable	15.00	18.00
Butter Dish & Cover	450.00	----
Candy in Metal Holder Motif on Lid Only	135.00	----
Creamer, Footed	11.50	12.50
Cup	7.00	7.50
Pitcher, 8½", 64 oz.	195.00	225.00
Plate, 6" Sherbet	3.00	4.50
Plate, 8⅜" Salad	6.00	7.00

	Green	Yellow
Plate, 9⅜" Luncheon	8.00	8.50
Plate, 10⅜" Dinner	16.00	18.00
Plate, 10⅜" Grill	25.00	25.00
Plate, 11¼" Sandwich . . .	10.00	12.00
Platter, 10¾" Oval	15.00	17.00
Relish, 3-Part, Footed	15.00	25.00
Saucer	3.00	3.50
Sherbet	10.00	11.50
Sugar, Open	10.00	10.50
Tumbler, 4¼", 9 oz.	75.00	----
Tumbler, 4¾", 12 oz.	85.00	----
Tumbler, 9 oz. Footed . . .	14.00	15.00
Tumbler, 12 oz. Footed . .	80.00	90.00

NO. 616, "VERNON"
(green, crystal, yellow)
INDIANA GLASS COMPANY, 1930-1932

	Green	Yellow		Green	Yellow
Creamer, Footed	20.00	17.50	Saucer	4.50	4.50
Cup	13.50	13.00	Sugar, Footed	19.50	17.50
Plate, 8" Luncheon	6.50	6.50	Tumbler, 5" Footed	25.00	25.00
Plate, 11" Sandwich	18.00	18.00			

NO. 618, "PINEAPPLE & FLORAL"
(crystal, amber, fired-on red)
INDIANA GLASS COMPANY, 1932-1937

	Crystal	Amber		Crystal	Amber
Ash Tray, 4½"	13.00	----	Plate, 9⅜" Dinner	10.00	12.50
Bowl, 4¾"	20.00	14.00	Plate, 11½" Sandwich ...	12.50	13.50
Bowl, 6" Cereal	18.50	16.00	Platter, 11" Closed Handles	10.00	12.00
Bowl, 7" Salad	5.00	8.50	Platter, Relish, 11½",		
Bowl, 10" Oval Vegetable	20.00	16.00	Divided	15.00	----
Compote, Diamond Shaped	1.50	6.50	Saucer	3.00	3.00
Creamer Diamond Shaped	6.50	9.00	Sherbet, Footed	15.00	15.00
Cream Soup	18.00	19.00	Sugar, Diamond Shaped .	6.50	8.50
Cup	7.50	7.00	Tumbler, 4¼", 8 oz.	25.00	----
Plate, 6" Sherbet	3.00	4.00	Tumbler, 5", 12 oz.	30.00	----
Plate, 8⅜" Salad	5.00	6.00	Vase, Cone Shaped, Large	30.00	----

NO. 622 "PRETZEL"
(crystal)
INDIANA GLASS COMPANY, 1930s

	Crystal		Crystal
Bowl, 4½" Fruit Cup	2.50	Plate, 6" Bread & Butter .	1.50
Bowl, 7" Olive, Leaf Shaped	2.50	Plate, 6" Tab Handled . . .	2.00
Bowl, 7½" Soup	7.50	Plate, 8⅜" Salad	3.00
Bowl, 8½", 2 Handled,		Plate, 9⅜" Dinner	4.00
Pickle	3.00	Plate, 11½" Sandwich	7.00
Bowl, 9⅜" Berry	10.00	Saucer	1.00
Bowl, 10¼" Celery	3.00	Sugar	3.50
Creamer	4.50	Tumbler, 5 oz. Juice	10.00
Cup	3.50	Tumbler, 9 oz. Water	12.00
Pitcher, 39 oz.	100.00	Tumbler, 12 oz.	15.00

OLD CAFE
(pink, crystal, ruby red)
HOCKING GLASS COMPANY, 1936-1938; 1940

	Pink	Red		Pink	Red
Bowl, 3¾" Berry	2.00	4.00	Pitcher, 80 oz	75.00	----
Bowl, 5", One or Two			Plate, 6" Sherbet	1.50	----
Handles	3.00	----	Plate, 10" Dinner	16.00	----
Bowl, 5½" Cereal	4.00	8.50	Saucer	1.50	----
Bowl, 9" Closed Handles	7.50	11.50	Sherbet, Low Footed	4.50	----
Candy Dish, 8" Low	5.00	10.00	Tumbler, 3" Juice	6.50	7.50
Cup	3.00	6.00	Tumbler, 4" Water	6.00	----
Lamp	12.50	20.00	Vase, 7¼"	9.50	13.50
Olive Dish, 6" Oblong	4.00	----			

OLD ENGLISH, "THREADING"
(green, pink, amber)
INDIANA GLASS COMPANY, Late 1920s

	All Colors		All Colors
Bowl, 4" Berry	12.00	Pitcher w/Cover	90.00
Bowl, 9" Footed Fruit	22.50	Plate, Indent for Compote	17.50
Bowl, 9½" Flat	25.00	Sandwich Server, Center	
✕ Candlesticks, 4", Pr.	22.50	Handle	40.00
Candy Jar w/Lid, Ftd.	40.00	Sherbet, 2 Styles	16.00
Candy & Lid, Flat	37.50	Sugar	12.00
Compote, 3½" Tall, 7"		Sugar Cover	25.00
Across	14.00	Tumbler, 4½" Footed	14.00
Creamer	14.00	Tumbler, 5½" Footed	25.00
Fruit Stand, 11" Footed	32.50	Vase, Fan 7"	35.00
Goblet, 5¾", 8 oz.	22.50	Vase, 12", Footed	40.00
Pitcher	50.00		

OVIDE, incorrectly dubbed "New Century"
(green, white, black)
HAZEL ATLAS GLASS COMPANY, 1930-1935

	Green	Black		Green	Black
Bowl, 4¾" Berry	----	7.00	Plate, 6" Sherbet	1.00	2.50
Bowl, 5½" Cereal	----	7.00	Plate, 8" Luncheon	1.50	6.00
Bowl, 8" Large Berry	----	14.00	Salt & Pepper, Pr.	10.00	22.50
Candy Dish & Cover	15.00	35.00	Saucer	1.25	2.00
Cocktail, Fruit, Footed	2.00	3.00	Sherbet	1.50	5.00
Creamer	2.50	5.00	Sugar, Open	2.50	5.00
Cup	2.00	5.00			

OYSTER and PEARL
(pink, crystal, ruby red, white with fired on pink or green)
ANCHOR HOCKING GLASS, 1938-1940

	Pink	Red		Pink	Red
Bowl, 5¼″ Round or Handled	5.00	9.50	Bowl, 10½″ Fruit, Deep . .	16.00	32.50
			Candleholder, 3½″, Pr. . . .	15.00	32.50
Bowl, 5¼″ Heart Shaped, One Handled	5.00	----	Plate, 13½″ Sandwich . . .	10.00	27.50
Bowl, 6½″ Deep, Handled	8.00	15.00	Relish Dish, 10¼″ Oblong	7.00	----

"PARROT," SYLVAN
(green, amber, crystal)
FEDERAL GLASS COMPANY, 1931-1932

	Green	Amber
Bowl, 5″ Berry	12.50	10.00
Bowl, 7″ Soup	27.50	25.00
Bowl, 8″ Large Berry	50.00	60.00
Bowl, 10″ Oval Vegetable	35.00	45.00
Butter Dish & Cover	245.00	950.00
Creamer, Footed	20.00	30.00
Cup	25.00	25.00
Hot Plate, 5″	500.00	----
Jam Dish, 7″	25.00	25.00
Pitcher, 8½″, 80 oz.	1000.00	----
Plate, 5¾″ Sherbet	17.50	11.00
Plate, 7½″ Salad	17.50	----
Plate, 9″ Dinner	30.00	25.00
Plate, 10½″ Grill, Round	20.00	----

	Green	Amber
Plate, 10½″ Grill, Square	----	17.50
Plate, 10¼″ Square	45.00	45.00
Platter, 11¼″ Oblong	27.50	45.00
Salt & Pepper, Pr.	195.00	----
Saucer	8.50	8.50
Sherbet, Footed, Cone	16.50	15.00
Sherbet, 4¼″ High	200.00	----
Sugar	20.00	25.00
Sugar Cover	95.00	300.00
Tumbler, 4¼″, 10 oz.	95.00	95.00
Tumbler, 5½″, 12 oz.	110.00	110.00
Tumbler, 5¾″ Footed, Heavy	97.50	110.00

PATRICIAN, "SPOKE"
(pink, green, amber, crystal)
FEDERAL GLASS COMPANY, 1933-1937

	Amber	Green		Amber	Green
Bowl, 4¾" Cream Soup . .	11.00	16.00	Plate, 9" Luncheon	7.50	7.00
Bowl, 5" Berry	7.50	8.50	Plate, 10½" Dinner	5.50	27.50
Bowl, 6" Cereal	17.00	19.00	Plate, 10½" Grill	9.00	10.00
Bowl, 8½" Large Berry . .	32.00	22.00	Platter, 11½" Oval	20.00	17.00
Bowl, 10" Oval Vegetable	20.00	20.00	Salt & Pepper, Pr.	42.50	45.00
Butter Dish & Cover	70.00	95.00	Saucer	6.50	5.00
Cookie Jar & Cover	65.00	300.00	Sherbet	9.00	10.00
Creamer, Footed	7.00	9.50	Sugar	6.50	7.00
Cup	6.50	8.50	Sugar Cover	35.00	42.50
Pitcher, 8", 75 oz.	85.00	90.00	Tumbler, 4", 5 oz.	23.00	25.00
Pitcher, 8¼", 75 oz.	100.00	110.00	Tumbler, 4½", 9 oz.	20.00	20.00
Plate, 6" Sherbet	7.00	6.00	Tumbler, 5½", 14 oz.	28.00	30.00
Plate, 7½" Salad	10.00	10.00	Tumbler, 5½", 8 oz. Footed	32.00	40.00

"PATRICK"
(yellow, pink)
LANCASTER GLASS COMPANY, EARLY 1930s

	Yellow/ Pink		Yellow/ Pink
Bowl, 9″ Handled Fruit . . .	20.00	Mayonnaise, 3 Pc.	40.00
Bowl, 11″ Console	25.00	Plate, 7″ Sherbet	5.00
X Candlesticks, Pr.	35.00	Plate, 7½″ Salad	6.00
Candy Dish, 3 Footed	32.50	Plate, 8″ Luncheon	6.50
Cheese & Cracker Set . . .	35.00	Saucer	2.00
Creamer	11.00	Sherbet, 4¾″	15.00
Cup	8.00	Sugar	10.00
Goblet, 4″ Cocktail	17.50	Tray, 11″, 2 Handled	17.50
Goblet, 4¾″, 6 oz. Juice .	18.00	Tray, 11″, Center Handled	25.00
Goblet, 6″, 10 oz. Water .	22.50		

PETALWARE
(pink, crystal, monax, cremax)
MacBETH-EVANS GLASS COMPANY, 1930-1940

	Pink	Monax		Pink	Monax
Bowl, 4½" Cream Soup ..	5.00	7.50	Plate, 6" Sherbet	1.00	2.00
Bowl, 5¾" Cereal	4.00	4.50	Plate, 8" Salad	1.75	3.00
Bowl, 8¾" Large Berry ..	8.00	13.00	Plate, 9" Dinner	4.50	4.00
Cup	2.50	4.50	Plate, 11" Salver........	5.00	6.50
Creamer, Footed	3.50	4.50	Platter, 13" Oval	9.00	12.00
Lamp Shade (Many Sizes)	----	7.50	Saucer	1.00	1.00
Mustard w/Metal Cover in			Sherbet, Low Footed	3.50	4.50
Cobalt Blue Only		5.00	Sugar, Footed	3.50	4.50

PRIMO, "PANELLED ASTER"
(green, yellow)
U.S. COMPANY, Early 1930s

	Yellow/Green		Yellow/Green
Bowl, 4½"	8.00	Plate, 10" Dinner	10.00
Bowl, 7¾"	15.00	Plate, 10" Grill	7.50
Cake Plate, 10", 3 Ftd.	15.00	Saucer	2.00
Coaster/Ash Tray	6.50	Sherbet	7.50
Creamer	7.50	Sugar	7.50
Cup	6.50	Tumbler, 5¾", 9 oz.	12.00
Plate, 7½"	5.00		

PRINCESS
(green, pink, topaz, apricot)
HOCKING GLASS COMPANY, 1931-1935

	Pink	Green		Pink	Green
Ash Tray, 4½"	57.50	60.00	Plate, 11½" Sandwich, Handled	7.50	10.00
Bowl, 4½" Berry	12.50	17.00	Platter, 12" Closed Handles	12.00	13.50
Bowl, 5" Cereal or Oatmeal	18.00	22.00	Relish, 7½" Divided	14.00	19.00
Bowl, 9" Salad Octagonal	20.00	25.00	Relish, 7½" Plain	----	70.00
Bowl, 9½" Hat Shaped	17.00	30.00	Salt & Pepper, 4½" Pr.	33.00	40.00
Bowl, 10" Oval Vegetable	15.00	18.00	Saucer (Same as Sherbet Plate)	3.50	5.50
Butter Dish & Cover	65.00	70.00			
Cake Stand, 10"	12.00	15.00	Sherbet, Footed	11.00	15.00
Candy Dish & Cover	37.50	35.00	Sugar	6.50	8.50
Coaster	55.00	25.00	Sugar Cover	12.00	13.50
Cookie Jar & Cover	40.00	35.00	Tumbler, 3", 5 oz. Juice	17.00	22.00
Creamer, Oval	9.00	10.00	Tumbler, 4", 9 oz. Water	14.00	20.00
Cup	6.50	9.00	Tumbler, 5¼", 13 oz. Iced Tea	16.50	25.00
Pitcher, 6", 37 oz.	30.00	35.00			
Pitcher, 7⅜", 24 oz. Footed	425.00	500.00	Tumbler, 4¾", 9 oz. Sq. Foot	45.00	55.00
Pitcher, 8", 60 oz.	35.00	37.50	Tumbler, 5¼", 10 oz. Footed	16.00	22.50
Plate, 5½" Sherbet	3.50	5.50			
Plate, 8" Salad	7.00	9.50	Tumbler, 6½" Footed, 12½ oz.	40.00	65.00
Plate, 9" Dinner	13.00	19.00	Vase, 8"	18.00	24.00
Plate, 9" Grill	7.00	10.00			
Plate, 11½" Grill, Closed Handles	7.00	9.00			

QUEEN MARY, "VERTICAL RIBBED"
(pink, crystal)
HOCKING GLASS COMPANY, 1936-1940

	Pink	Crystal		Pink	Crystal
Ash Tray, Oval, 2"x3¾" .	3.50	2.00	Compote, 5¾"	9.00	5.00
Bowl, 4" One Handle or			Creamer, Oval	5.00	4.00
None	4.00	2.50	Cup	5.00	4.50
Bowl, 5" Berry, 6" Cereal	10.00	4.00	Plate, 6" & 6⅝"	2.50	2.00
Bowl, 5½", Two Handles .	5.00	3.00	Plate, 8½" Salad	5.00	3.50
Bowl, 8¾" Large Berry . .	10.00	6.00	Plate, 9¾" Dinner	20.00	11.00
Butter Dish or Preserve &			Plate, 12" Sandwich	10.00	6.00
Cover	90.00	20.00	Plate, 14" Serving Tray . .	15.00	9.00
Candy Dish & Cover	25.00	15.00	Relish Tray, 12", 3-Part . .	10.00	8.00
Candlesticks, 4½" Double			Relish Tray, 14", 4-Part . .	10.00	8.00
Branch, Pr.	----	14.00	Salt & Pepper, Pr.	15.00	----
Celery or Pickle Dish,			Saucer	1.50	1.00
5"x10"	15.00	7.00	Sherbet, Footed	4.00	3.50
Cigarette Jar, Oval 2"x3" .	5.50	3.50	Sugar, Oval	5.00	4.00
Coaster, 3½"	2.50	2.00	Tumbler, 3½", 5 oz. Juice	6.00	3.00
Coaster/Ash Tray, 4¼"			Tumbler, 4", 9 oz. Water .	5.50	4.00
Square	4.50	4.00	Tumbler, 5", 10 oz. Footed	25.00	22.00

RADIANCE
(red, cobalt and ice blue, amber, crystal)
NEW MARTINSVILLE, 1936-1939

	Red Blue	Other Colors		Red Blue	Other Colors
Bonbon, 6″	12.00	7.50	Creamer...............	12.50	9.50
Bonbon, 6″ Footed	13.00	8.50	Cruet, Individual	45.00	30.00
Bonbon, 6″ Covered	35.00	16.00	Cup	10.00	8.00
Bowl, 5″, 2 Handled, Nut .	14.00	7.50	Decanter, Handled		
Bowl, 7″, 2-Part.........	13.00	7.50	w/Stopper	125.00	75.00
Bowl, 7″ Pickle	12.50	10.00	Lamp, 12″	72.50	42.50
Bowl, 8″, 3-Part Relish ...	22.50	15.00	Mayonnaise, 3 Pc. Set ...	30.00	17.50
Bowl, 10″ Celery........	15.00	10.00	Pitcher, 64 oz..........	175.00	125.00
Bowl, 10″ Crimped	22.50	15.00	Plate, 8″ Luncheon......	8.00	6.00
Bowl, 10″ Flared	22.50	15.00	Plate, 14″ Punch Bowl Liner	45.00	22.00
Bowl, 12″ Crimped	27.50	17.50	Punch Bowl	135.00	75.00
Bowl, 12″ Flared	27.50	17.50	Punch Cup, Flat	8.00	5.00
Butter Dish	350.00	140.00	Punch Ladle	100.00	75.00
Candlestick, 8″, Pr.	45.00	27.50	Salt & Pepper, Pr.......	60.00	40.00
Candle, 2 Light, Pr.	50.00	35.00	Saucer	5.00	3.50
Cheese & Cracker, 11″ Plate			Sugar	14.00	10.00
Set	30.00	17.50	Tray, Oval	25.00	20.00
Comport, 5″............	10.00	6.50	Tumbler, 9 oz...........	20.00	12.50
Comport, 6″............	12.50	7.50	Vase, 10″ Flared........	35.00	22.50
Condiment Set, 4 Pc. on			Vase, 12″ Crimped	65.00	40.00
Tray	130.00	95.00			

RAINDROPS, "OPTIC DESIGN"
(green, crystal)
FEDERAL GLASS COMPANY, 1929-1933

	Green		Green
Bowl, 4½" Fruit	3.00	Salt & Pepper, Pr.	150.00
Bowl, 6" Cereal	4.00	Saucer	1.00
Bowl, 7½" Berry	25.00	Sherbet	5.00
Cup	4.00	Sugar	4.50
Creamer	5.00	Sugar Cover	30.00
Plate, 6" Sherbet	1.50	Tumbler, 3", 4 oz.	3.50
Plate, 8" Luncheon	3.50	Whiskey, 1⅞"	4.00

RIBBON
(green, black, crystal)
HAZEL ATLAS GLASS COMPANY, 1930-1932

	Green	Black		Green	Black
Bowl, 4" Berry	4.00	----	Salt & Pepper, Pr.	17.50	35.00
Bowl, 8" Large Berry	13.50	17.50	Saucer	1.00	----
Candy Dish & Cover	27.50	----	Sherbet, Footed	4.00	----
Creamer, Footed	10.00	----	Sugar, Footed	9.00	----
Cup	3.50	----	Tumbler, 5½", 10 oz.	10.00	----
Plate, 6¼" Sherbet	1.50	----	Tumbler, 6½", 13 oz.	16.00	----
Plate, 8" Luncheon	3.00	10.00			

RING, "BANDED RINGS"
(crystal, green and crystal with decoration)
HOCKING GLASS COMPANY, 1927-1932

	Crystal	Green, Dec.		Crystal	Green, Dec.
Bowl, 5″ Berry	2.50	3.50	Saucer	1.25	1.50
Bowl, 7″ Soup	7.50	10.00	Sherbet, Low (for 6½″		
Bowl, 8″ Large Berry	5.00	7.50	Plate)	4.00	10.00
Butter Tub or Ice Bucket	10.00	17.50	Sherbet, 4¾″ Footed	4.00	7.50
Cocktail Shaker	10.00	17.50	Sugar, Footed	3.00	4.00
Cup	3.00	3.50	Tumbler, 3½″, 5 oz.	2.50	4.00
Creamer, Footed	3.50	4.50	Tumbler, 4¼″, 9 oz.	3.50	4.00
Decanter & Stopper	15.00	25.00	Tumbler, 5⅛″, 12 oz.	4.00	5.00
Goblet, 7″ to 8″, (Varies),			Tumbler, 3½″ Footed		
9 oz.	6.00	12.50	Cocktail	4.00	5.00
Ice Tub	12.00	17.50	Tumbler, 5½″ Footed		
Pitcher, 8″, 60 oz.	10.00	15.00	Water	4.00	6.00
Pitcher, 8½″, 80 oz.	12.00	20.00	Tumbler, 6½″ Footed Iced		
Plate, 6¼″ Sherbet	1.25	1.50	Tea	5.00	10.00
Plate, 6½″ Off Center Ring	1.50	4.50	Vase, 8″	12.50	27.50
Plate, 8″ Luncheon	1.50	3.00	Whiskey, 2″, 1½ oz.	3.50	5.50
*Salt & Pepper, 3″, Pr.	15.00	25.00			
Sandwich Server Center					
Handle	12.00	20.00			

*Green — $55.00

ROCK CRYSTAL,
"EARLY AMERICAN ROCK CRYSTAL"
(pink, green, cobalt, red, yellow, amber, blue-green, crystal)
McKEE GLASS COMPANY, 1920s and 1930s in color

	Crystal	Red		Crystal	Red
*Bonbon, 7½", S.E.	15.00	40.00	Candlesticks, 8½" Tall,		
Bowl, 4", 5" Fruit, S.E.	8.00	20.00	Pr.	60.00	185.00
**Bowl, 5" Finger Bowl w/7"			Candy & Cover, Round .	28.00	135.00
Plate, P.E.	15.00	37.50	Cake Stand, 11" Footed,		
Bowl, 7" Pickle or Spoon			2¾" High	20.00	85.00
Tray	17.50	50.00	Compote, 7"	27.50	55.00
Bowl, 7", 8" Salad, S.E.	17.50	45.00	Creamer, 9 oz. Footed .	15.00	50.00
Bowl, 9", 10½" Salad,			Cruet & Stopper, 6 oz. Oil	50.00	----
S.E.	20.00	65.00	Cup, 7 oz.	12.00	55.00
Bowl, 11½" Two-Part			Goblet, 7½" oz., 8 oz.		
Relish	27.00	50.00	Low Footed	13.50	45.00
Bowl, 12" Oblong Celery	20.00	47.50	Goblet, 11 oz. Low Footed		
Bowl, 12½" Footed			Iced Tea	15.00	55.00
Center Bowl	40.00	210.00	Jelly, 5" Footed, S.E. . .	13.50	37.50
Bowl, 13" Roll Tray . . .	25.00	----	Lamp, Electric	85.00	350.00
Bowl, 14" Six-Part Relish	25.00	----	Parfait, 3½ oz. Low Foot	15.00	60.00
Candelabra, Two Lite, Pr.	35.00	175.00	Pitcher, ½ Gal., 7½"		
Candelabra, Three Lite,			High	85.00	----
Pr.	40.00	200.00	Pitcher, Large	125.00	500.00
Candlesticks, 5½" Low,			Plate, 6" Bread & Butter,		
Pr.	27.50	100.00	S.E.	4.50	12.50

	Crystal	Red
Plate, 7½", 8½" Salad, P.E. & S.E.	6.50	17.50
Plate, 9", 10½", 11½" Cake, S.E. (small center design)	12.50	45.00
Plate, 10½" Dinner, S.E. (large center design)	40.00	110.00
Salt & Pepper, 2 styles	65.00	----
Salt Dip	25.00	----
Sandwich Server Center Handled	20.00	85.00
Saucer	5.00	12.50
Sherbet or Egg, 3½ oz., Footed	12.00	50.00
Stemware, 1 oz., Footed Cordial	22.50	50.00
Stemware, 2 oz., 3 oz., Footed Wines	16.00	45.00
Stemware, 3½ oz., Footed Cocktail	12.00	35.00

	Crystal	Red
Stemware, 6 oz., Footed Champagne	12.50	28.00
Stemware, 8 oz. Large Footed Goblet	13.50	45.00
Sundae, 6 oz. Low Footed	9.50	28.00
Sugar, 10 oz. Open, Flat	17.50	----
Sugar, 10 oz. Covered, Footed	30.00	85.00
Tumbler, 2½" oz., Whiskey	12.50	40.00
Tumbler, 5 oz. Juice	12.00	40.00
Tumbler, 5 oz. Old Fashioned	12.00	35.00
Tumbler, 9 oz. Concave or Straight	15.00	40.00
Tumbler, 12 oz. Concave or Straight	20.00	50.00
Vase, 11" Footed	40.00	125.00

*S.E. — McKee designation for scalloped edge
**P.E. — McKee designation for plain edge

ROSE CAMEO
(green)
BELMONT TUMBLER COMPANY, 1931

	Green		Green
Bowl, 4½" Berry	4.50	Sherbet	8.00
Bowl, 5" Cereal	8.00	Tumbler, 5" Footed	
Bowl, 6" Straight Side	11.00	(2 styles)	11.00
Plate, 7" Salad	5.50		

ROSEMARY, "DUTCH ROSE"
(pink, green, amber)
FEDERAL GLASS COMPANY, 1935-1937

	Amber	Green		Amber	Green
Bowl, 5″ Berry	4.00	5.00	Plate, Dinner	5.50	10.00
Bowl, 5″ Cream Soup	8.00	14.00	Plate, Grill	6.00	10.00
Bowl, 6″ Cereal	15.00	20.00	Platter, 12″ Oval	9.50	15.00
Bowl, 10″ Oval Vegetable	9.00	20.00	Saucer	2.00	3.50
Creamer, Footed	6.50	9.00	Sugar, Footed	6.50	9.50
Cup	4.00	7.00	Tumbler, 4¼″, 9 oz.	20.00	22.50
Plate, 6¾″ Salad	4.00	6.00			

ROULETTE, "MANY WINDOWS"
(pink, green)
HOCKING GLASS COMPANY, 1935-1939

	Pink	Green		Pink	Green
Bowl, 9" Fruit	----	10.00	Tumbler, 3¼", 7½ oz. Old		
Cup	----	4.25	Fashioned	8.00	17.50
Pitcher, 8", 64 oz.	22.50	25.00	Tumbler, 4⅛", 9 oz. Water	10.00	12.50
Plate, 6" Sherbet	----	2.25	Tumbler, 5⅛", 12 oz. Iced		
Plate, 8½" Luncheon	----	4.00	Tea	10.00	16.50
Plate, 12" Sandwich	----	7.50	Tumbler, 5½", 10 oz.		
Saucer	----	2.25	Footed	10.00	15.00
Sherbet	----	4.50	Whiskey, 2½", 1½ oz.	6.50	9.00
Tumbler, 3¼", 5 oz. Juice	6.00	9.50			

"ROUND ROBIN"
(green, iridescent)
1927-1932

	Green	Irides-cent		Green	Irides-cent
Bowl, 4" Berry	4.25	4.00	Plate, 8" Luncheon	2.50	3.00
Cup, Footed	4.00	5.00	Plate, 12" Sandwich	5.00	6.00
Creamer, Footed	5.00	5.50	Saucer	1.50	1.50
Domino Tray	25.00	----	Sherbet	4.00	5.00
Plate, 6" Sherbet	1.50	1.50	Sugar	4.50	5.00

ROXANA
(yellow, white, crystal)
HAZEL ATLAS GLASS COMPANY, 1932

	Yellow		Yellow
Bowl, 4½"x2⅜"	6.00	Saucer	2.50
Bowl, 5" Berry..........	4.00	Sherbet, Footed	4.00
Bowl, 6" Cereal.........	6.50	Tumbler, 4", 9 oz........	10.00
Plate, 6" Sherbet	2.50		

ROYAL LACE
(pink, green, crystal, blue)
HAZEL ATLAS GLASS COMPANY, 1934-1941

	Pink	Blue		Pink	Blue
Bowl, 4¾" Cream Soup . .	12.00	24.00	Pitcher, 48 oz., Straight		
Bowl, 5" Berry	18.00	30.00	Sides	42.00	85.00
Bowl, 10" Round Berry . .	18.00	40.00	Pitcher, 8", 68 oz.	50.00	120.00
Bowl, 10", 3 Leg, Straight			Pitcher, 8", 86 oz.	55.00	135.00
Edge	20.00	42.50	Pitcher, 8½", 96 oz.	65.00	165.00
Bowl, 10", 3 Leg, Rolled			Plate, 6" Sherbet	3.50	8.50
Edge	27.50	225.00	Plate, 8½" Luncheon	8.50	23.00
Bowl, 10", 3 Leg, Ruffled			Plate, 10" Dinner	12.00	27.50
Edge	25.00	300.00	Plate, 9⅞" Grill	10.00	22.50
Bowl, 11" Oval Vegetable	18.00	38.00	Platter, 13" Oval	18.00	40.00
Butter Dish & Cover	120.00	425.00	Salt & Pepper, Pr.	42.00	200.00
Candlesticks, Pr., Straight			Saucer	3.50	7.50
Edge	28.00	77.50	Sherbet, Footed	9.00	27.50
Candlesticks, Pr., Rolled			Sugar	9.00	21.00
Edge	38.00	110.00	Sugar Lid	22.50	100.00
Candlestick, Pr., Ruffled			Tumbler, 3½", 5 oz.	15.00	30.00
Edge	35.00	105.00	Tumbler, 4⅛", 9 oz.	11.00	26.00
Cookie Jar & Cover	37.50	235.00	Tumbler, 4⅞", 10 oz.	27.50	55.00
Creamer, Footed	12.00	27.50	Tumbler, 5⅜", 12 oz.	27.50	45.00
Cup	9.00	23.50			

ROYAL RUBY
(red)
ANCHOR HOCKING GLASS COMPANY, 1939-1960s

	Red		Red
Ash Tray, 4½" Square . . .	2.50	Plate, 9" or 9¼" Dinner . .	7.50
Bowl, 4¼" Berry	4.00	Plate, 13¾"	15.00
Bowl, 5¼"	8.00	Punch Bowl & Stand	32.50
Bowl, 7½" Soup	9.50	Punch Cup	2.00
Bowl, 8" Oval Vegetable .	27.50	Saucer (Round or Square)	1.50
Bowl, 8½" Large Berry . .	12.50	Sherbet, Footed	6.50
Bowl, 10" Deep	17.50	Sugar, Flat	6.00
Bowl, 11½" Salad	20.00	Sugar, Footed	5.00
Card Holder	35.00	Sugar Lid	8.00
Creamer, Flat	6.00	Tumbler, 2½" Footed Wine	10.00
Creamer, Footed	7.50	Tumbler, 3½" Cocktail . . .	7.50
Cup (Round or Square) . .	3.50	Tumbler, 5 oz. Juice, 2	
Goblet, Ball Stem	7.00	Styles	5.00
Lamp	20.00	Tumbler, 9 oz. Water	5.00
Pitcher, 22 oz., Tilted or		Tumbler, 10 oz. Water . . .	5.00
Upright	20.00	Tumbler, 13 oz. Iced Tea .	9.50
Pitcher, 3 Qt., Tilted	25.00	Vase, 4" Ball Shaped	4.50
Pitcher, 3 Qt., Upright . . .	30.00	Vase, 6½" Bulbous, Tall .	7.50
Plate, 6½" Sherbet	2.00	Vases, Several Styles (small)	5.00
Plate, 7" Salad	3.50	Vases, Several Styles (large)	10.00
Plate, 7¾" Luncheon	4.00		

"S" PATTERN, "STIPPLED ROSE BAND"
(crystal, amber)
MacBETH-EVANS GLASS COMPANY, 1930-1933

	Crystal	Amber		Crystal	Amber
Bowl, 5½" Cereal	2.50	3.50	Plate, 11" Heavy Cake . . .	30.00	35.00
Bowl, 8½" Large Berry . .	7.50	12.50	Plate, 13" Heavy Cake . . .	50.00	60.00
Creamer, Thick or Thin . .	4.00	5.50	Saucer	1.00	1.50
Cup, Thick or Thin	2.50	3.50	Sherbet, Low Footed	3.50	6.00
Pitcher, 80 oz.	37.50	75.00	Sugar, Thick & Thin	4.00	5.50
Plate, 6" Sherbet	1.50	2.00	Tumbler, 3½", 5 oz.	2.50	4.50
Plate, 8" Luncheon	3.50	2.50	Tumbler, 4", 9 oz.	3.50	5.50
Plate, 9¼" Dinner	3.50	6.50	Tumbler, 4¼", 10 oz.	3.50	6.00
Plate, Grill	5.00	6.50	Tumbler, 5", 12 oz.	7.50	10.00

SANDWICH
(See Reproduction Section, Page 150)
(crystal, 1930-1960s; amber [desert gold], 1960s; pink & ruby red, 1939-1940; forest green, 1950s-1960s; white [opaque], 1950s)
HOCKING GLASS COMPANY, 1939-1964

	Crystal	Green		Crystal	Green
Bowl, 4⅞" Berry	4.00	2.00	Pitcher, 6" Juice	42.50	90.00
Bowl, 6" Cereal	18.00	----	Pitcher, ½ gal., Ice Lip	45.00	185.00
Bowl, 6½" Smooth or			Plate, 7" Dessert	8.00	----
Scalloped	6.00	27.50	Plate, 8"	3.00	----
Bowl, 7" Salad	6.50	40.00	Plate, 9" Dinner	11.00	49.50
Bowl, 8" Smooth or			Plate, 9" Indent for Punch		
Scalloped	6.50	45.00	Cup	3.00	----
Bowl, 8¼" Oval	6.00	----	Plate, 12" Sandwich	9.00	----
Butter Dish, Low	32.50	----	Saucer	1.00	6.00
Cookie Jar & Cover	30.00	----	Sherbet, Footed	6.00	----
Creamer	4.50	15.00	Sugar & Cover	12.50	15.00*
Cup, Tea or Coffee	1.75	15.00	Tumbler, 5 oz. Juice	5.00	2.75
Custard Cup	3.50	1.50	Tumbler, 9 oz. Water	6.50	3.25
Custard Cup Liner	7.50	1.25	Tumbler, 9 oz. Footed	16.50	----

*(No Lid)

SANDWICH
(See Reproduction Section, Page 151)
(crystal, amber, pink, red, teal blue, light green)
INDIANA GLASS COMPANY, 1920-1970s

	Crystal	Pink		Crystal	Pink
Ash Tray Set (Club, Spade, Heart, Diamond Shapes) each	2.00	----	Pitcher, 68 oz.	45.00	75.00
Bowl, 4¼" Berry	3.00	3.00	Plate, 6" Sherbet	1.25	2.50
Bowl, 6"	3.50	3.50	Plate, 7" Bread & Butter	1.50	3.00
Bowl, 6", 6 Sides	3.00	3.50	Plate, 8" Oval, Indent for Sherbet	2.50	3.50
Bowl, 8¼"	10.00	10.00	Plate, 8⅜" Luncheon	2.50	4.00
Bowl, 9" Console	15.00	15.00	Plate, 10½" Dinner	8.00	12.00
Bowl, 10" Console	15.00	18.00	Plate, 13" Sandwich	6.00	10.00
Butter Dish & Cover, Domed	65.00	150.00	Sandwich Server, Center Handle	20.00	25.00
Candlesticks, 3½", Pr.	15.00	13.00	Saucer	1.50	2.00
Candlesticks, 7", Pr.	38.00	35.00	Sugar	4.00	6.00
Creamer	6.50	6.00	Tumbler, 3 oz. Footed Cocktail	15.00	----
Cruet, 6½" & Stopper	37.50	----	Tumbler, 8 oz. Footed Water	10.00	----
Cup	4.50	4.00	Tumbler, 12 oz. Footed Iced Tea	12.00	----
Creamer & Sugar on Diamond Shaped Tray	14.00	----	Wine, 3", 4 oz.	17.00	----
Decanter & Stopper	40.00	65.00			
Goblet, 9 oz.	11.00	12.00			

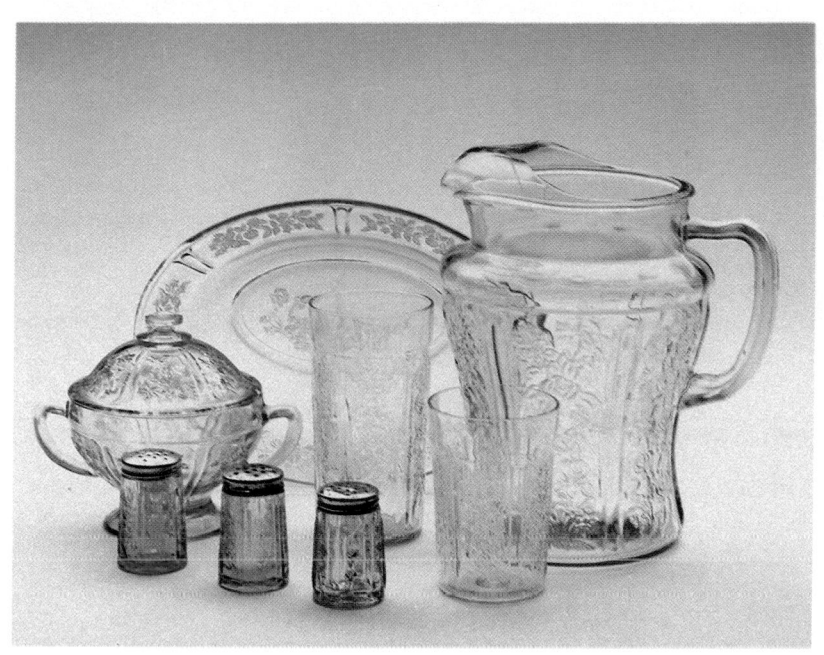

SHARON, "CABBAGE ROSE"
(See Reproduction Section, Page 152)
(pink, green, amber, crystal)
FEDERAL GLASS COMPANY, 1935-1939

	Amber	Pink
Bowl, 5″ Berry	6.00	7.00
Bowl, 5″ Cream Soup	17.50	30.00
Bowl, 6″ Cereal	11.00	15.00
Bowl, 7½″ Flat Soup, Two Inches Deep	27.50	27.50
Bowl, 8½″ Large Berry	4.50	16.00
Bowl, 9½″ Oval Vegetable	10.00	16.00
Bowl, 10½″ Fruit	15.00	22.00
Butter Dish & Cover	40.00	35.00
Cake Plate, Footed, 11½″	16.00	24.00
Candy Jar & Cover	35.00	33.00
Cheese Dish & Cover	160.00	600.00
Creamer, Footed	10.00	11.00
Cup	8.00	9.00
Jam Dish, 7½″	25.00	100.00
Pitcher, 80 oz. With or Without Ice Lip	100.00	95.00

	Amber	Pink
Plate, 6″ Bread & Butter	3.00	3.00
Plate, 7½″ Salad	11.00	16.50
Plate, 9½″ Dinner	9.50	10.00
Platter, 12½″ Oval	12.00	13.50
Salt & Pepper, Pr.	32.50	32.50
Saucer	4.00	5.50
Sherbet, Footed	9.00	10.00
Sugar	6.50	9.50
Sugar Lid	17.50	17.50
Tumbler, 4⅛″, 9 oz. Thick or Thin	21.00	20.00
Tumbler, 5¼″, 12 oz. Thick or Thin	28.00	32.50
Tumbler, 6½″ Footed, 15 oz.	65.00	32.50

SIERRA, ''PINWHEEL''
(pink, green)
JEANNETTE GLASS COMPANY, 1931-1933

	Pink	Green		Pink	Green
Bowl, 5½" Cereal	7.00	8.00	Platter, 11" Oval	25.00	30.00
Bowl, 8½" Large Berry . .	10.00	15.00	Salt & Pepper, Pr.	27.50	30.00
Bowl, 9½" Oval Vegetable	25.00	50.00	Saucer	3.50	4.00
Butter Dish & Cover	45.00	50.00	Serving Tray, 2 Handles . .	9.50	10.00
Creamer	10.00	14.00	Sugar	12.50	15.00
Cup	7.50	9.00	Sugar Cover	10.00	10.00
Pitcher, 6½", 32 oz.	45.00	75.00	Tumbler, 4½", 9 oz. Footed	32.00	50.00
Plate, 9" Dinner	10.50	13.00			

SPIRAL
(green)
HOCKING GLASS COMPANY, 1928-1930

	Green		Green
Bowl, 4¾" Berry	4.00	Preserve & Cover	20.00
Bowl, 7" Mixing	6.00	Salt & Pepper, Pr.	17.50
Bowl, 8" Large Berry	7.50	Sandwich Server, Center	
Creamer, Flat or Footed	5.00	Handle	17.50
Cup	4.00	Saucer	1.00
Ice or Butter Tub	15.00	Sherbet	3.00
Pitcher, 7⅝", 58 oz.	24.00	Sugar, Flat or Footed	5.00
Plate, 6" Sherbet	1.00	Tumbler, 3", 5 oz. Juice	2.75
Plate, 8" Luncheon	2.50	Tumbler, 5", 9 oz. Water	4.00

STARLIGHT
(pink, white, crystal)
HAZEL ATLAS GLASS COMPANY, 1938-1940

	Crystal	Pink		Crystal	Pink
Bowl, 5½" Cereal	3.00	5.00	Plate, 9" Dinner	4.00	----
Bowl, 8½" Closed Handles	4.00	9.00	Plate, 13" Sandwich	7.50	8.50
Bowl, 11½" Salad	14.00	----	Relish Dish	9.00	----
Plate, 6" Bread & Butter	2.00	----	Salt & Pepper, Pr.	16.00	----
Creamer, Oval	3.00	----	Saucer	1.00	----
Cup	2.50	----	Sherbet	8.00	----
Plate, 8½" Luncheon	2.50	----	Sugar, Oval	3.00	----

STRAWBERRY
(pink, green, iridescent)
U.S. GLASS COMPANY, 1928-1931

	Pink or Green		Pink or Green
Bowl, 4″ Berry	7.00	Pickle Dish	10.00
Bowl, 6¼″, 2″ Deep	40.00	Pitcher, 7¾″	135.00
Bowl, 6½″ Deep Salad	15.00	Plate, 6″ Sherbet	5.00
Bowl, 7½″ Deep Berry	14.00	Plate, 7½″ Salad	9.00
Butter Dish & Cover	125.00	Sherbet	6.50
Compote, 5¾″	13.00	Sugar, Small, Open	12.50
Creamer, Small	12.50	Sugar, Large	15.00
Creamer, Large, 4⅝″	17.50	Sugar Cover	30.00
Olive Dish, 5″, One Handle	10.00	Tumbler, 3⅝″, 9 oz.	22.50

SUNFLOWER
(pink, green)
JEANNETTE GLASS COMPANY, Late 1920s

	Pink	Green		Pink	Green
Ash Tray, 5" Center Design Only	7.00	7.00	Saucer	3.00	4.00
Cake Plate, 10", 3 Legs	9.00	9.00	Sugar	12.00	13.00
Creamer	12.50	13.50	Tumbler, 4¾", 8 oz. Footed	15.00	20.00
Cup	8.00	9.00	Trivet, 7", 3 Legs, Turned Up Edge	175.00	195.00
Plate, 9" Dinner	9.00	12.00			

SWIRL, "PETAL SWIRL"
(pink, ultra-marine, delphite)
JEANNETTE GLASS COMPANY, 1937-1938

	Pink	Ultra-marine		Pink	Ultra-marine
Ash Tray, 5⅜"	6.00	----	Plate, 6½" Sherbet	2.50	3.50
Bowl, 5¼" Cereal	5.50	8.00	Plate, 7¼"	4.50	7.50
Bowl, 9" Salad	9.50	15.00	Plate, 8" Salad	6.00	9.50
Bowl, 10" Footed, Closed			Plate, 9¼" Dinner	7.00	10.00
Handles	----	22.50	Plate, 12½" Sandwich	7.50	14.00
Bowl, 10½" Console,			Salt & Pepper, Pr.	----	27.50
Footed	14.00	20.00	Saucer	1.50	2.00
Butter Dish	135.00	200.00	Sherbet, Low Footed	6.00	10.00
Candleholders, Double			Soup - Tab Handles (Lug)	12.50	16.00
Branch, Pr.	----	25.00	Sugar, Footed	6.50	9.50
Candy Dish, Open, 3 Legs	6.00	8.50	Tumbler, 4", 9 oz.	8.00	15.00
Candy Dish w/Cover	55.00	75.00	Tumbler, 5⅛", 13 oz.	16.00	45.00
Coaster, 1"x3¼"	5.50	7.50	Tumbler, 9 oz. Footed	12.50	18.00
Creamer, Footed	6.50	9.50	Vase, 6½" Footed	11.50	15.00
Cup	5.00	8.50	Vase, 8½" Footed	----	17.50
Pitcher, 48 oz., Footed	----	975.00			

TEA ROOM
(green, pink)
INDIANA GLASS COMPANY, 1926-1931

	Green	Pink		Green	Pink
Bowl, Finger	35.00	30.00	Plate, 8¼" Luncheon	25.00	22.50
Bowl, 7½" Banana Split..	60.00	60.00	Plate, 10½", Two Handled	40.00	35.00
Bowl, 8½" Celery	25.00	20.00	Relish, Divided	16.00	13.00
Bowl, 8¾" Deep Salad ..	65.00	50.00	Salt & Pepper, Pr........	40.00	37.50
Bowl, 9½" Oval Vegetable	45.00	40.00	Saucer	15.00	15.00
Candlestick, Low, Pr.	35.00	30.00	Sherbet, Three Styles	16.00	14.00
Creamer, 4"	12.50	10.00	Sugar, 4"	13.50	10.00
Creamer & Sugar on Tray,			Sugar, Flat w/Cover	90.00	80.00
3½"	50.00	50.00	Sundae, Footed, Ruffled..	75.00	60.00
Cup	27.50	25.00	Tumbler, 8½ oz., Flat....	75.00	65.00
Goblet, 9 oz.	60.00	50.00	Tumbler, 6 oz., Footed ...	25.00	25.00
Ice Bucket	40.00	35.00	Tumbler, 9 oz., Footed ...	22.00	20.00
Lamp, 9" Electric	35.00	30.00	Tumbler, 11 oz., Footed ..	32.50	27.50
Mustard, Covered	95.00	85.00	Tumbler, 12 oz., Footed ..	40.00	35.00
Parfait	50.00	45.00	Vase, 9"	50.00	40.00
Pitcher, 64 oz.	100.00	95.00	Vase, 11" Ruffled Edge or		
Plate, 6½" Sherbet	20.00	18.00	Straight	70.00	65.00

THISTLE
(pink, green)
MacBETH-EVANS, 1929-1930

	Pink	Green		Pink	Green
Bowl, 5½" Cereal	12.00	16.00	Plate, 10¼" Grill	12.50	15.00
Bowl, 10¼" Large Fruit . .	185.00	125.00	Plate, 13" Heavy Cake . . .	85.00	95.00
Cup, Thin	14.00	17.50	Saucer	7.50	7.50
Plate, 8" Luncheon	8.00	12.50			

TWISTED OPTIC
(pink, green, amber, crystal)
IMPERIAL GLASS COMPANY, 1927-1930

	Pink or Green		Pink or Green
Bowl, 4¾" Cream Soup . .	7.00	Preserve (Same as Candy but w/slot in lid)	17.50
Bowl, 5" Cereal	3.00		
Bowl, 7" Salad or Soup . .	6.00	Sandwich Server, Center Handle	15.00
Candlestick, 3", Pr.	12.00		
Candy Jar & Cover	17.50	Sandwich Server, Two Handled Flat	6.00
Creamer	6.00		
Cup	2.50	Saucer	1.00
Pitcher, 64 oz.	17.50	Sherbet	4.00
Plate, 6" Sherbet	1.50	Sugar	5.00
Plate, 7" Salad	2.00	Tumbler, 4½", 9 oz.	4.50
Plate, 7½"x9" Oval	4.00	Tumbler, 5¼", 12 oz.	6.50
Plate, 8" Luncheon	2.00		

U.S. SWIRL
(pink, green)
U.S. GLASS COMPANY, Late 1920s

	Green	Pink		Green	Pink
Bowl, 4⅜" Berry	4.50	5.00	Creamer	10.00	11.00
Bowl, 5½" One Handled	8.50	9.00	Pitcher, 8", 48 oz.	30.00	40.00
Bowl, 7⅛" Large Berry	11.00	12.00	Plate, 6⅛" Sherbet	1.50	1.75
Bowl, 8¼" Oval	12.50	13.50	Plate, 7⅞" Salad	4.50	5.00
Butter & Cover	55.00	70.00	Salt & Pepper, Pr.	30.00	35.00
Butter Bottom	42.50	52.50	Sherbet, 3¼"	3.50	4.00
Butter Top	10.00	15.00	Sugar w/lid	25.00	30.00
Candy w/Cover, Two			Tumbler, 4⅝", 12 oz.	8.50	9.00
Handled	20.00	22.50	Vase, 6½"	12.50	13.50

"VICTORY"
(amber, green, pink, cobalt blue)
DIAMOND GLASS-WARE COMPANY, 1929-1932

	Pink	Blue		Pink	Blue
Bonbon, 7"	9.00	15.00	Gravy Boat & Platter	135.00	250.00
Bowl, 6½" Cereal	7.50	18.00	Mayonnaise Set: 3½" Tall,		
Bowl, 8½" Flat Soup	10.00	25.00	5½" Across, 8½" In-		
Bowl, 9" Oval Vegetable .	25.00	45.00	dented Plate w/Ladle...	35.00	65.00
Bowl, 11" Rolled Edge ...	20.00	35.00	Plate, 6" Bread & Butter .	3.00	8.00
Bowl, 12" Console	27.50	----	Plate, 7" Salad	5.50	10.00
Bowl, 12½" Flat Edge ...	22.50	50.00	Plate, 8" Luncheon	5.00	12.50
Candlesticks, 3", Pr......	25.00	65.00	Plate, 9" Dinner	12.50	22.50
Cheese & Cracker Set, 12"			Platter, 12"	17.50	45.00
Indented Plate & Compote	25.00	----	Sandwich Server, Center		
Comport, 6" Tall, 6¾"			Handle	20.00	45.00
Diameter..............	10.00	----	Saucer	2.00	6.00
Creamer...............	10.00	30.00	Sherbet, Footed	10.00	17.50
Cup	6.00	20.00	Sugar	10.00	30.00
Goblet, 5", 7 oz.	17.50	----			

VITROCK ("FLOWER RIM")
(white)
ANCHOR HOCKING GLASS COMPANY, 1934-late 1930s

	White		White
Bowl, 4" Berry	3.50	Plate, Salad, 7¼"	1.50
Bowl, Cream Soup, 5½"	8.00	Plate, Luncheon, 8¾"	2.00
Bowl, Fruit, 6"	4.00	Plate, Soup, 9"	7.00
Bowl, Cereal, 7½"	3.00	Plate, Dinner, 10"	4.00
Bowl, Vegetable	7.00	Platter, 11½"	17.50
Creamer, Oval	3.00	Saucer	1.00
Cup	2.00	Sugar, Oval	3.00

WATERFORD, "WAFFLE"
(crystal, pink)
HOCKING GLASS COMPANY, 1938-1944

	Crystal	Pink		Crystal	Pink
Ash Tray, 4"	6.00	----	Plate, 7⅛" Salad	2.00	4.50
Bowl, 4¾" Berry	4.00	7.00	Plate, 9⅝" Dinner	5.00	11.00
Bowl, 5½" Cereal	9.00	14.00	Plate, 10¼" Handled Cake	5.00	9.50
Bowl, 8¼" Large Berry . .	6.00	12.50	Plate, 13¾" Sandwich . . .	5.00	20.00
Butter Dish & Cover	22.00	175.00	Salt & Pepper, 2 Types . .	8.50	----
Coaster, 4"	2.00	5.00	Saucer	1.00	3.50
Creamer, Oval	2.50	7.50	Sherbet, Footed	2.50	7.00
Cup	3.50	10.00	Sugar	2.50	6.50
Goblet, 5¼", 5⅝"	12.00	----	Sugar Cover, Oval	2.50	17.50
Pitcher, 42 oz. Juice, Tilted	17.50	----	Tumbler, 4⅞", 10 oz.		
Pitcher, 80 oz. Ice Lip, Tilted	25.00	100.00	Footed	8.50	12.00
Plate, 6" Sherbet	1.75	3.50	Vase, 6¾"	8.50	----

WINDSOR, "WINDSOR DIAMOND"
(pink, green, crystal)
JEANNETTE GLASS COMPANY, 1932-1946

	Crystal	Pink		Crystal	Pink
Ash Tray, 5¾"	11.50	30.00	Plate, 6" Sherbet	1.50	3.50
Bowl, 4¾" Berry	2.50	5.00	Plate, 7" Salad	3.00	10.00
Bowl, 5" Cream Soup. . . .	4.50	12.50	Plate, 9" Dinner	3.00	9.50
Bowl, 5⅛", 5⅜" Cereals .	5.00	11.00	Plate, 10¼" Sandwich,		
Bowl, 7⅛", Three Legs . .	6.00	15.00	Handled	4.00	10.00
Bowl, 8½" Large Berry . .	4.50	10.00	Plate, 13⅝" Chop	7.50	20.00
Bowl, 9½" Oval Vegetable	5.00	12.00	Platter, 11½" Oval	4.50	11.00
Bowl, 12½" Fruit Console	20.00	65.00	Relish Platter, 11½" Divided	7.50	7.00
Bowl, 7"x11¾" Boat Shape	12.00	20.00	Salt & Pepper, Pr.	12.50	37.50
Butter Dish	22.50	37.50	Saucer	1.50	3.00
Cake Plate, 13½" Thick. .	6.50	11.50	Sherbet, Footed	2.50	7.00
Candlesticks, 3", Pr.	15.00	55.00	Sugar & Cover.	4.50	17.50
Candy Jar & Cover	10.00	25.00	Tray, 4" Square	2.50	6.50
Coaster, 3¼"	2.50	7.00	Tray, 4⅛"x9"	3.00	7.50
Compote	3.50	12.00	Tray, 8½"x9¾"	6.00	20.00
Creamer.	3.00	7.50	Tumbler, 3¼", 5 oz.	6.00	20.00
Cup	2.50	6.00	Tumbler, 4", 9 oz.	5.00	17.50
Pitcher, 4½", 16 oz.	17.50	95.00	Tumbler, 5", 12 oz.	7.50	27.50
Pitcher, 6¾", 52 oz.	11.00	18.50	Tumbler, 7¼" Footed	9.00	----

135

"ADAM"
Privately produced out of Korea through St. Louis Importing Company

The new Adam butter is being offerd at $6.50 wholesale. Identification of the new is easy.

TOP: Notice the veins in the leaves.
NEW: Large leaf veins do not join or touch in center of leaf.
OLD: Large leaf veins all touch or join center vein on the old.

A further note in the original Adam butter dish the veins of all the leaves at the center of the design are very clear cut and precisely moulded, whereas in the new these center leaf veins are very indistinct - and almost invisible in open leaf of the center design.

BOTTOM: Place butter dish bottom upside down for observation.
NEW: Four (4), "Arrowhead-like" points line up in the northwest, northeast, southeast and southwest directions of compass.
OLD: Four (4) "Arrowhead-like" points line up in north, east, south and west directions of the compass.

There are very bad mold lines and very glossy light pink color on those butter dishes I have examined but these could be improved.

NEW "AVOCADO"
(pink, frosted pink, yellow, blue, red, amethyst, frosted green)
INDIANA GLASS COMPANY, Tiara Exclusives Line, 1974

Thus far, the company has only overlapped the original glass colors in pink and only the pitcher and tumbler sets have been made. The original pink color is lighter in shade than this newer, slightly orange tint, pink.

Some of these sets, such as red, were made in limited editions as a selling point with buyers who are hopeful that someday they may be more valuable. Perhaps they shall, but I personally feel it will take many years for these to have more than their original value.

CHERRY BLOSSOM
(pink, green, blue, delphite, red cobalt blue, various iridized colors)
PRIVATELY PRODUCED 1973. . .

In 1973 the Depression Glass world was stunned with the appearance of a child's butter dish nd some odd looking child's cups—odd because no child's butter dish was made originally and because in the bottoms of the cups, the cherry design was hanging upside down. Since then, the upside down design has been rectified and some saucers and plates have appeared. However, all these pieces haven't the sveltness of the original pieces and are easily spotted.

In 1977 butter dishes and shakers appeared. Some shakers in pink and green were dated '77; other pink, green and delphite shakers appeared non dated. These shakers are readily recognizable by the almost squared protrusions around the top edge of the shakers. I call them helicopter blades. On the original shakers these protrusions are more rounded and they extend only slightly outward from the top. If you wish to carry your examinations further than that, the design on the shakers is weaker in spots on the newer versions.

The butter dishes pose a bit more problem in distinguishing old from new except in the pretty blue color which wasn't an original color. However, if you use your tactile sense and feel the design inside the butter top, you will find it very sharply defined in the new; also, the knob on the new top is very sharply defined whereas in the old, the knob is more smoothly formed.

Again, about ½″ from the edge of the new top, you will notice one band. In the old, there are two distinct bands to be noted there.

I could write a book on the differences between old and new scalloped bottom, AOP Cherry pitchers. The easiest way to tell the differences is to turn the pitcher over. My old Cherry pitcher has nine cherries on th bottom. The new one only has seven. Further, the branch crossing the bottom of my old Cherry pitcher LOOKS like a branch. It's knobby and gnarled and has several leaves and cherry stems directly attached to it. The new pitcher just has a bald strip of glass halving the bottom of the pitcher. Further, the old cherry pitchers have a plain glass background for the cherries and leaves in the bottom of the pitcher. In the new pitchers, there's a rough, filled in, straw-like background. You see no plain glass. (My new Cherry pitcher just cracked sitting in a box by my typing stand -- another tendency which I understand is common to the new)!

As for the new tumblers, the easiest way to tell old from the new is to look at the ring dividing the patterned portion of the glass from the plain glass lip. The old tumblers have three indented rings dividing the pattern from the plain glass rim. The new has only one. (Turn back and look at the red cherry tumbler pictured with Cherry Blossom pattern). Further, as in the pitcher, the arching encircling the cherry blossoms on the new tumblers is very sharply ridged. On the old tumblers, that arching is so smooth you can barely feel it. Again, the pattern at the bottom of the new tumblers is brief and practically nonexistent in the center curve of the glass bottom. This was sharply defined on most of the old tumblers. You can see how far toward the edge the pattern came on the red cherry tumbler pictured with the pattern. The pattern, what there is, on the new tumblers mostly hugs the center of the foot.

Several different people have gotten into the act of making reproduction Cherry Blossom. We've even enjoyed some reproductions of reproductions! All the items pictured on the next pages are extremely easy to spot as reproductions (colors never made!) once you know what to look for with the possible exception of the 13″ divided platter pictured at the back. It's too heavy, weighing 2¾ pounds and has a thick, ⅜″ of glass in the bottom; but the design isn't too bad! The edges of the leaves aren't smooth; but neither are they serrated like old leaves.

Now for a quick run down of the various items.

The Cherry child's dishes were first made in 1973.

First to appear was a child's cherry cup with a slightly lop-sided handle and having the cherries hanging upside down when the cup was held in the right hand. (This defiance of gravity was due to the inversion of the design when the mold, taken from an original cup, was inverted to create the outside of the "new" cup). After I reported this error, it was quickly corrected by re-inverting the inverted mold. These later cups were thus improved in design but slightly off color. The saucers tended to have slightly off center designs, too. Next came the "child's butter dish" which was never made by Jeannette. It was essentially the child's cup without a handle turned upside down over the saucer and having a little blob of glass added as a knob for lifting purposes. You could get this item in pink, green, light blue, cobalt, gray-green and iridescent carnival colors. A blue one is pictured on the next page.

2 handled tray - old: 1⅞ lbs.; ³⁄₁₆″ glass in bottom; leaves and cherries east/west from north/south handles; leaves have real spine and serrated edges; cherry stems end in triangle of glass.

2 handled tray - new: 2⅛ lbs.; ¼″ glass in bottom; leaves and cherries north/south with the handles; canal type leaves (but uneven edges); cherry stem ends before cup shaped line.

cake plate - new: color too light pink, leaves have too many parallel veins which give them a "feathery" look; arches at plate edge don't line up with lines on inside of the rim to which the feet are attached.

8½″ bowl - new: crude leaves with smooth edges; veins in parallel lines.

cereal bowl - new: wrong shape, looks like 8½″ bowl, 2″ center.

cereal bowl - old: large center, 2½″ inside ring, nearly 3½″ if you count the outer rim before the sides turn up.

plate - new: center shown close up; smooth edged leaves, fish spine type center leaf portion; weighs 1 pound plus; feels thicker at edge with mold offset lines clearly visible. (See next page).

plate - old: center leaves look like real leaves with spines, veins, & serrated edges; weighs ¾ pound; clean edges; no mold offset.

cup - new: area in bottom left free of design; canal leaves; smooth, thick top to cup handle (old has triangle grasp point)

saucer - new: off set mold line edge; canal leaf center.

NEW "MADRID"
(amber, pink, crystal, blue)
FEDERAL GLASS COMPANY, 1976-1977, 1980s

Introduced by Federal as "Recollection" in 1976 ostensibly for the Bi-Centennial. Each piece is dated '76 as shown here on a plate edge. The color is a deeper amber than the old.

The butter dish knob has mold marks running from north to south on the new; the mold marks run east to west on the old. I mention this only because on occasion new tops are "married" to old bottoms in an attempt to do a bit of "wool pulling". In my area, the starter sets are now down to $9.95 and still not selling, whereas the butter dish is sold out.

Other items introduced in 1977 are candleholders, creamer and sugar with no lid, a footed candy and cover, a footed square bowl and a footed cake plate. These last three footed pieces are not duplicates of the original Madrid. However, due to the first issues not selling so well, many stores failed to stock these latter pieces.

Indiana Glass is at it again. They continue to issue glass in colors made originally. Instead of creating new collectibles in colors never made, they insist in wiping out many a collector's dreams of financial profit by remaking glassware long discontinued. Shown at the top on the right is the "new" Recollection Pink Madrid. Thankfully, not much pink was made in the 1930s when Federal made Madrid. The picture at the top shows new concepts in design that were never made. There are other pedestal pieces using the candlestick for the base besides the cake plate shown. Once you have seen the pale, washed-out pink on any of these items, you will never have trouble spotting these culprits.

The bottom picture shows glassware similar to that made in the 1930s but of those, only the oval vegetable and cup and saucer were made by Federal. The original pink is deep like Sharon's pink. Although, I omitted showing the candlesticks, the new ones have ridges inside the opening to grasp the candle while the older did not. I might add that the candles have shown up in BLACK.

A special thanks to John and Trannie Davis for furnishing this "Recollection" for this book. The better department stores were the first to have these items, but the discount houses are now advertising them so you will see a lot of this in pink, crystal and blue as time goes by.

Blue has been made in all of the pieces shown in pink. It is a vivid blue when compared to the older subtle shade "Madonna Blue" made by Federal originally.

NEW "MAYFAIR"

**(pink, green, blue, cobalt [shot glasses], 1977 onward.
pink, green, "brownish" amethyst [cookie jars], 1982; pink, cobalt blue
[shakers] 1988.)**

Mayfair cookie jars, at cursory glance, have a base of which has a very indistinct design. It will feel smooth to the touch, its so faint. In the old cookie jars, there's a distinct pattern which feels like raised embossing to the touch. Next, turn the bottom upside down. The new bottom is perfectly smooth. The old bottom contains a 1¾" mold circle rim that Is raised enough to catch your fingernail in it. There are other distinctions as well; but that is the quickest way to tell old from new.

In the Mayfair cookie lid, the new design (parallel to the straight side of the lid) at the edge curves gracefully toward the center "V" shape (rather like bird wings in flight); in the old, that edge is flat, straight line going into the "V" (like airplane wings sticking straight out from the side of the plane as you face it head on).

The green color of the cookie, as you can see from the picture, is not the pretty, yellow/green color of true green Mayfair. It also doesn't "glow" under black light as the old green does.

So, you see, none of these reproductions give us any trouble; they're all easily spotted by those of us now "in the know"!

Only the shot glass (which is rare in the original) has been made in this pattern. The green (totally wrong color) and blue are no problem since the shot glasses have never been found in these colors originally. The difficulty comes with the pink.

Generally speaking, the newer shot glass has a heavier over-all look. The bottom area tends to have a thicker rim of glass. Often, the "pink" coloring isn't right; it may be too light, it may be too orange. However, if these cursory examinations fail, there are other points to check.

First, notice the stem of the flower. You have a single stem in the new flower. At the base of the stem in the old glass, the stem separates into an "A" shape. Further, look at the leaves on the stem. In the new design, the leaf itself is hollow with the veins molded in. In the old glass, the leaf portion is molded in and the veining is left hollow. In the center of the flower, the dots (anther) cluster entirely to one side of the old design and are rather distinct. Nothing like that occurs in the newer version.

Repro Mayfair Shaker

	Old	New
*Diameter of opening	¾"	⅝"
Diameter of lid	⅞"	¾"
Height	4¹⁄₁₆"	4"
Corner Ridges on Shaker	Rise ½ way to top then smooth out	Rise to top & are quite pro-nounced

* Most immediately noticeable factor.

Thanks to Millie and Bill Downey for the use of the blue Mayfair shakers.

NEW "MISS AMERICA"
(crystal, green, pink, ice blue, red amberina)
PRIVATELY PRODUCED 1977 . . .

The new butter dish in "Miss America" design is probably the best of the newer products; yet there are three distinct differences to be found between the original butter top and the newly made one. Since the value of the butter dish lies in the top, it seems more profitable to examine it.

In the new butter dishes pictured, notice that the panels reaching the edge of the butter bottom tend to have a pronounced curving, skirt-like edge. In the original dish, there is much less curving at the edge of these panels.

Second, pick up the top of the new dish and feel up inside it. If the butter top knob is filled with glass so that it is convex (curve outward), the dish is new; the old inside knob area is concave (curved inward).

Finally, from the underside, look through the top toward the knob. In the original butter dish you would see a perfectly formed multi-sided star; in the newer version, you see distorted rays with no visible points.

Shakers have been made in green, pink and crystal. The shakers will have new tops; but since some old shakers have been given new tops, that isn't conclusive at all. Unscrew the lid. Old shakers have a very neatly formed ridge of glass on which to screw the lid. If it overlaps a little and has neatly rounded off ends. Old shakers stand 3⅜" tall without the lid. New ones stand 3¼" tall. Old shakers have almost a forefinger's depth inside (female finger) or a fraction shy of 2½ inches. New shakers have an inside depth of 2", about the second digit bend of a female's finger. (I'm doing finger depths since most of you will have those with you at the flea market, rather than a tape measure). In men, the old shaker's depth covers my knuckle; the new shaker leaves my knuckle exposed. New shakers simply have more glass on the inside of the shaker--something you can spot from twelve feet away - the hobs are more rounded on the newer shaker, particularly near the stem and seams; in the old shaker these areas remained pointedly sharp!

New Miss America tumblers have ½" of glass in the bottom, has a smooth edge on the bottom of the glass with no mold rim and show only two distinct mold marks on the sides of the glass. Old tumblers have only ¼" of glass in the bottom, have a distinct mold line rimming the bottom of the tumbler and have four distinct mold marks up the sides of the tumbler. The new green tumbler doesn't "glow" under black light as did the old.

New Miss America pitchers are all perfectly smooth rimmed at the top edge above the handle. All old pitchers that I have seen have a "hump" in the top rim of the glass above the handle area, rather like a camel's hump. The very bottom diamonds next to the foot in the new pitchers "squash" into elongated diamonds. In the old pitchers, these get noticeably smaller, but they retain their diamond shape.

SANDWICH
(crystal)
ANCHOR HOCKING GLASS COMPANY

At present, only the cookie jar has been re-introduced to use the jargon of today. However, we may assume that if sales are good for this item, we will see others. The newer jar is much larger when compared with the old.

	New	Old
Height	10¼"	9¼"
Opening Width	5½"	4⅞"
Diameter/Largest Part	22"	19"

SANDWICH
(amber, blue, red, green)
INDIANA GLASS COMPANY, Tiara Exclusive Line 1969 . . .

In recent years Sandwich in amber, the smokey blue shown here and a sprayed red over crystal have been issued. In 1969 came red in quite a few pieces and these are difficult to tell from the older pieces of the 1930s. Any piece you see in amber or blue is of recent origin.

Bad news for collectors came in 1978 when Tiara announced that they were going to issue the Sandwich in crystal from decanter sets down to the domed butter dish. My advice here is to be wary of paying any high prices for the old at this time. Since the original molds are being used, there is little difference.

SHARON
(blue, dark green, light green, pink, burnt umber)
PRIVATELY PRODUCED 1976 . . .

A blue Sharon butter turned up in 1976 and created a sensation. The blue was the color of Mayfair blue; but this color was unknown in Sharon pattern. This fluke helped to quickly inform Depression enthusiasts that new editions were being made available.

In similar colors, you can distinguish between the old and the new butter dishes by noticing that the bottom ridge of the newer butter dish is sharply defined; the old bottom ledge is barely defined. Also, the top of the newer butter dish is heavier and thicker than the old—in most instances, it even weighs more. The knob is easier to grasp on the new butter dishes as it sticks up higher and you've more room to fit your finger around the knob and grasp the top. In the old butter dish tops, the knob fits so closely to the top that it makes it hard to grasp the knob.

In 1977 a "cheese dish" appeared having the same top as the butter. I put the name in quotes because it is but a parody of the original cheese dish. The new bottom of the dish is about half way between a flat plate and butter dish bottom and is over thick giving it an awkward appearance. The real cheese dish bottom more nearly resembles a salad plate with a raised rim. These "cheese dishes" are easily spotted as being new.

The newest reproduction in Sharon is a too light pink creamer and sugar with lid. They are pictured with their "Made in Taiwan" label. These sell for around $15.00 for the pair and are also easy to spot as reproductions. I'll just mention the most obvious differences. Turn the creamer so you are looking directly at the spout. In the old creamer the mold line runs dead center of that spout; in the new, the mold line runs decidedly to the left of center spout.

On the sugar, the leaves and roses are "off" but not enough to DESCRIBE it to new collectors. Therefore, look at the center design, both sides, at the stars located at the very bottom of the motif. A thin leaf stem should run directly from that center star upward on BOTH sides. In this new sugar, the stem only runs from one; it stops way short of the star on one side. OR look inside the sugar bowl at where the handle attaches to the bottom of the bowl. In the new bowl, this attachment looks like a perfect circle; in the old, its an upside down "v" shaped tear drop.

As for the sugar lid, the knob of the new lid is perfectly smooth as you grasp its edges. The old knob has a mold seam running mid circumference. You could tell these two lids apart blind folded!

While there is a hair's difference between the height, mouth opening diameter, and inside depth of the old Sharon shakers and those newly produced, I won't attempt to upset you with those sixteenth and thirty seconds of a degree of difference. Suffice it to say that in physical shape, they are very close. However, as concern design, they're miles apart. The old shakers have true appearing roses. The flowers really LOOK like roses. On the new shakers, they look like poorly drawn circles with wobbly concentric rings. The leaves are not as clearly defined on the new shakers as the old. However, forgetting all that, in the old shakers, the first design you see below the lid is a ROSE BUD. It's angled like a rocket shooting off into outer space with three leaves at the base of the bud (where the rocket fuel would burn out). In the new shakers, this "bud" has become four paddles of a windmill. It's the difference between this and this.

The shakers wholesale for around $6.50 a pair.

A Sharon candy dish has just been made by the infamous St. Louis group. It is very crude, thick and should pose no problems. Be aware that it does exist and *know your dealer.*

AUTHOR'S COMMENTS ON REPRODUCTIONS

As popularity of any item in the collecting field grows, there is always someone or some company that will take advantage of the collector. This section will show you the reproductions in Depression Glass through May, 1986.

Know your glassware or your dealer before spending your hard earned cash for it; also, be wary of deals that seem too good to be true.

The items pictured in this section have all been reproduced since 1973 either by the original glass companies themselves or by private individuals.

Items introduced by companies are usually available in the local dish barns or merchant stores. Those privately manufactured are found at flea markets or local antique or junk shops.

Some of the glass is marketed through private sales or parties much like the "Tupperware" patries. In these, the buyer is treated to "exclusive lines" of glassware.

My personal feeling is that as long as people buy these reproductions, re-issues, new products made to look old, or what have you, then they will continue to be made either privately or by the companies themselves. I feel also that buying a collectible is an investment; but buying a reproduction is merely speculation. These latter products appeal to me as much as swamp land in Florida.

What can we do? First, we can educate ourselves to know glass; secondly, we can refrain from buying the newer glass. Barring that, we who know the reproductions can label them as such when the opportunity arises.

Glossary of Terms

Amber—brownish yellow color (see Madrid or Patrician picture for example).

Amethyst—a light, pastel purple as opposed to black amethyst which appears black until held to strong light whereby it shows deep purple.

Apricot—a dark yellow color, yet lighter in shade than amber; usually used to desribe the darker shade of Princess than topaz.

A O P—abbreviation for "all over pattern" usually used to describe Cherry Blossom.

Berry Bowl—term used by many glass companies to desribe a round bowl.

BonBon—a candy dish, usually uncovered.

Bread and Butter Plate—usually a six inch plate in a pattern that does not have a sherbet.

Cake Plate—a heavy, flat plate, usually having 3 legs.

Carnival—older, iridized glassware from early 1900s; also term used to describe the color of Floragold or an iridized pattern.

Celery—usually a long, narrow, flat dish; in Colonial, a two handled dish taller than the sugar.

Cheese Dish—a covered dish, the bottom of which is normally flatter than that of the butter dish.

Chigger Bite—a term auctioneers use to describe a small chip on a dish.

Chop Plate—a large, flat plate called a salver by some companies.

Chunked—a polite way to describe a badly damaged piece of glass.

Claret—a goblet of varying size depending upon company terminology.

Closed Handled—having solid tab handles.

Coaster—glass liner sometimes doubling as an ash tray.

Cobalt Blue—a deep, dark blue color (shown in Moderntone or Moondrops).

Comport/Compote—term used to denote small, open candy dish which is stemmed.

Concentric Rings—circles within circles; gradually increasing or decreasing sized circles.

Console Bowl—centerpiece bowl, usually with candlesticks.

Cordial—goblet of varying size depending upon company terminology.

Cracker Jar—term for what would be a modern day cookie jar; they were sold with certain brands of products packed inside them.

Cream Soup—a two handled bouillon or consomme dish.

Decanter—usually a stoppered bottle for wine.

Delphite—a light blue opaque color; sometimes referred to as "blue milk glass".

Demitasse—a smaller than normal cup with saucer.

Domino Tray—a tray with a ring for creamer to reside in; the remaining surface within the tray being meant to hold sugar cubes.

Ebony—black color.

Etched—design cut into glass; usually found on better quality glass.

Fired-On—color applied and baked on at the factory.

Flashed-On—color added over crystal; usually wears off as opposed to the fired-on color which does not wear off with use.

Flat—a non footed dish; dish without a footed base or stem.

Fluted—scalloped edge.

Frog—heavy glass holed flower stem holder.

Goblet—a stemmed, bowl shaped tumbler.

Gravy Boat—oval shaped bowl used for serving gravy; often with a type of spout.

Grill Plate—a usually tri-sectioned plate of the type used in restaurants to keep the meat and vegetables divided from each other.

Hat Shaped—bowl looking like an up-turned hat.

Hot Plate—glass plate used for setting hot items on the table as a protection for the table or table spread.

Ice Blue—very light, crystal blue color.

Ice Bucket—a milk bucket like container for holding ice cubes.

Ice Lip—a guard or fold moulded about the lip of a pitcher to keep ice from falling out into the glass when pouring from the pitcher.

Jadite—an opaque, light green color.

Jam Jar—small, covered jar for holding jam or preserves.

Luncheon Plate—usually an 8-9 inch plate, smaller than a dinner plate.

Mayonnaise—an open, cone shaped compote.

Milk Glass—a white glassware, the color of milk, usually heavy.

Mold/Mould—a usually two part encasement into which hot glass is poured and a glass object is formed; depression glass was primarily a glassware made from molds rather than being blown or formed by hand.

Monax—white color produced by MacBeth Evans, usually very thin.

Motif—the pattern or design on glass.

Mug—a heavy cup, usually flat bottomed.

Nappy—old word denoting a bowl.

Opalescent—white rimmed flowing into color.

Open Handled—handles having an opening for the finger or hand to reach through.

Parfait—a tall, ice cream dish of the type used for sundaes in soda fountains of by-gone days.

Pickle Dish—an oblong dish used for serving pickles; smaller than a celery.

Platinum Band—an applied silver colored rim on glassware.

Platonite—Hazel Atlas heat resistant white glass often colored by a fired-on process.

Platter—oblong or oval shaped meat dish.

Preserve Dish—tall, footed dish often used as a candy.

Rayed—arrows or spoke-like designs on glass bottoms.

Relish—oblong dish, sometimes referred to as a pickle dish.

Rolled Edge—glassware having an edge curved in toward or out away from center.

Rope Edge—glassware with an edge having a rope-like design embedded in it.

Rose Bowl—small, curved in edged bowl, usually having a small center hole and usually tri-footed.

Salad Plate—usually 7-7½ inch plate, for serving salads.

Salver—large, 11-12 inch, non handled serving plate.

Sandwich Server—a salver or sometimes a handled, often center handled, serving plate.

S A S E—short for self addressed, stample envelope.

Sherbet—small, usually footed, ice cream or dessert dish.

Teal—a blue-green color in all companies except Jeannette.

Tid-Bit—a two or three tiered serving dish made of increasingly smaller plates connected by a center metal pole, around 12-15 inches tall.

Topaz—bright yellow colored glassware.

Trivet—a three footed hot plate, usually about 7 inches in diameter; similar in design to three footed cake plates but much smaller in diameter.

Tumbler—a glass.

Tumble Up—a glass bottle with long neck having a small tumbler seated up-side down over the bottle neck serving as the bottle top; usually used on night stand by bed to quinch night time thirst.

Ultra-Marine—Jeannette's blue-green color.

Vaseline—a glowing yellow colored glassware similar to the color of the jelly-like substance of the same name.

Additional Books By Gene Florence

Collector's Encyclopedia of Depression Glass, $19.95
Collector's Encyclopedia of Occupied Japan II, $14.95
Collector's Encyclopedia of Occupied Japan III, $19.95
Kitchen Glassware of the Depression Years, $19.95
Elegant Glassware of the Depression Era, $19.95
Very Rare Glassware of the Depression Years, $24.95

Add $1.50 postage for the first book, $.45 for each additional book.

Copies of these books may be ordered from:
Gene Florence, P.O. Box 22186, Lexington, KY 40522
or
COLLECTOR BOOKS, P.O. Box 3009, Paducah, KY 42001

Schroeder's Antiques Price Guide

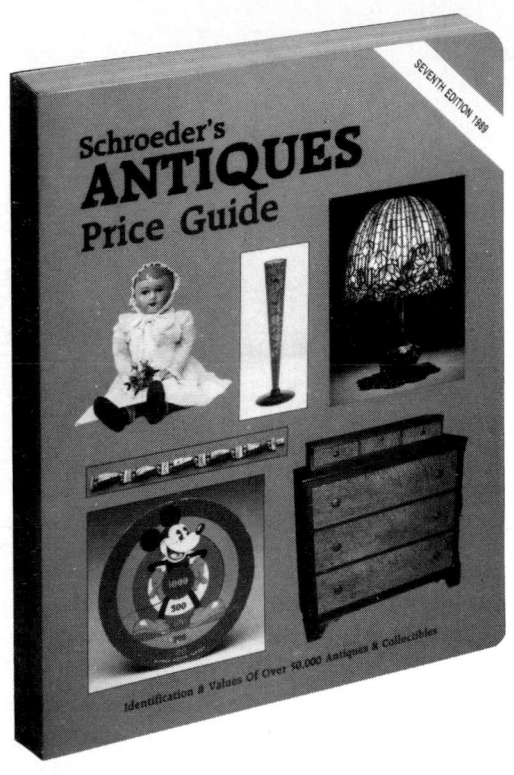

Schroeder's Antiques Price Guide has climbed its way to the top in a field already supplied with several well-established publications! The word is out, *Schroeder's Price Guide* is the best buy at any price. Over 500 categories are covered, with more than 50,000 listings. From ABC Plates to Zsolnay, if it merits the interest of today's collector, you'll find it in Schroeder's. Each subject is represented with histories and background information. In addition, hundreds of sharp original photos are used each year to illustrate not only the rare and the unusual, but the everyday "fun-type" collectibles as well. All new copy and all new illustrations make Schroeder's THE price guide on antiques and collectibles. We have not and will not simply change prices in each new edition.

The writing and researching team is backed by a staff of more than seventy of Collector Books' finest authors, as well as a board of advisors made up of well-known antique authorities and the country's top dealers, all specialists in their fields. Prices are gathered over the entire year previous to publication, then each category is thoroughly checked. Only the best of the lot remains for publication. You'll find the new edition of *Schroeder's Antiques Price Guide* the one to buy for factual information and quality.

No dealer, collector or investor can afford not to own this book. It is available from your favorite bookseller or antiques dealer at the low price of $12.95. If you are unable to find this price guide in your area, it's available from Collector Books, P.O. Box 3009, Paducah, KY 42001 at $12.95 plus $2.00 for postage and handling.